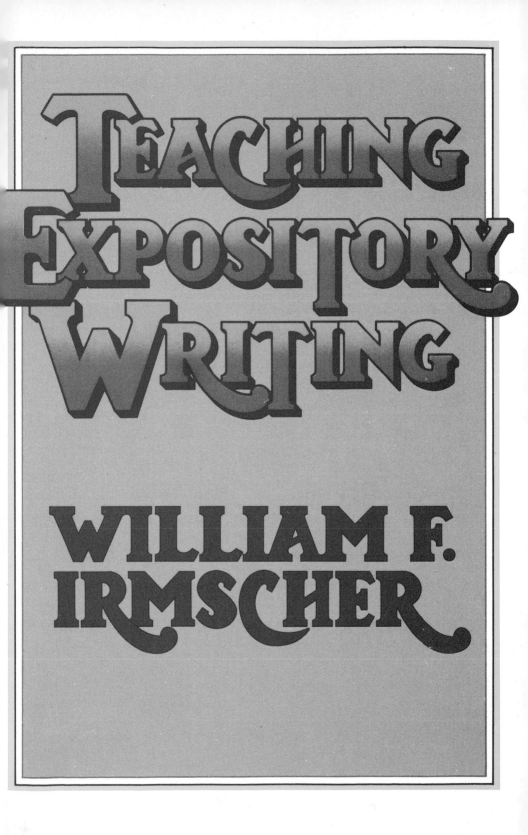

TEACHING EXPOSITORY WRITING

WILLIAM F. IRMSCHER

TEACHING EXPOSITORY WRITING

TEACHING EXPOSITORY WRITING

William F. Irmscher
University of Washington

HOLT, RINEHART AND WINSTON
New York   Chicago   San Francisco   Atlanta   Dallas
Montreal   Toronto   London   Sydney

Library of Congress Cataloging in Publication Data

Irmscher, William F
  Teaching expository writing.

  Includes index.
  1. English language—Rhetoric- Study and teaching. I. Title.
PE1404.I7   808'.042   78-13302

ISBN 0-03-044671-6

9 0 1 2 3   059   9 8 7 6 5 4 3 2

Preface

Writing brings thought into consciousness—our own and that of those who read. Much more information is available, but what we finally select to write about is what we consider meaningful and instructive. Thus, what I have written here about teaching is both a culmination or rather long teaching experience and a condensation. I have attempted to say only those things that I think teachers engaged in the teaching of writing should consider. No one can adopt exactly someone else's way. But as teachers we should share certain values, one of the most important and obvious of which is that students should learn.

Good teachers—those who make a difference—are rare. If we can count more than five in our own individual school experience, we are fortunate indeed. Teachers of writing are often among those who make a difference to students, chiefly because the one-to-one interaction is also far too scarce in school experiences. If that close relationship is reinforced by empathy and positive regard for the student, something valuable is bound to happen. That is simply the chemistry of teaching.

This book has run a gamut of six reviewers, and it has not emerged unaltered. Those reviewers are in no way to be identified with the views expressed here, because some of them clearly differed with my approaches. But they have helped both by their encouragement and challenges and by their focus on passages that needed expansion or stylistic revision. Their suggestions have, I am sure, made the book sounder and more readable. For the help they have given, I am indebted to Professors Richard S. Beal, Boston University; Michael C. Flanigan, Indiana University; Robert M. Gorrell, University of Nevada; Richard Lloyd-Jones, University of Iowa; Celia Millward, Boston University; Joseph Williams, University of Chicago.

In addition, I am grateful to Mr. Kenney Withers of Holt, Rinehart and Winston for his continuing support, to Ms. Pamela Forcey of Holt for her careful copy editing, and to Ms. Shirley Hanson, my secretary, who has become an indispensable part of the process of my writing, because she patiently types and retypes my many revisions. Finally, I am especially grateful to hundreds of teaching assistants through the years from whom I continue to learn about teaching. Many of them have been far better teachers of writing than I am. The only credit I take is that I recognize that fact and draw upon their fresh resources whenever I can.

W.F.I.

Contents

TEACHING EXPOSITORY WRITING

Introduction

I take the teaching of writing seriously. That statement doesn't mean I disclaim humor or support the notion that teaching composition is a joyless activity. But it does mean that I would like to see teachers treat the teaching of writing with a professional attitude. The teaching of writing is such a common, free-style undertaking in both our secondary schools and colleges that it may seem presumptuous of me to think that I can nudge it in the direction of professionalism by a book of this kind. I don't intend to write a day-by-day, how-to-do-it book, although I hope what I write has practical value to the extent that it makes clear what is involved in learning to write and what an instructor might best do to help students develop as writers.

In this book, I use "expository writing" as an umbrella term to mean simply writing that explains. In that sense, it includes various kinds of writing that are sometimes considered separate modes. But in practice they are not separate. Expository writing tends to be an amalgam. We sometimes explain by narrating, by describing, by defining, by reasoning, and, in the course of writing, perhaps arguing and persuading. Thus, in these terms, expository writing includes a broad range of nonfiction prose from factual reporting to personal reminiscence. I have excluded from consideration various forms of technical, scientific, and business writing, not because they are less important kinds of expository prose, but because they often involve forms and elements of style different from those discussed here. They need to be treated separately, although it is interesting to note the growing tendency among some teachers to recognize flexible forms, personal voice, and stylistic variation as permissible elements in technical and scientific writing.

I am addressing both inexperienced and experienced teachers. Initiates, I am convinced, ordinarily know much more about the teaching of writing than they think they do. In many instances, they may need to be reminded of things they have forgotten; in others, to test the soundness of what they know. And, finally, both inexperienced and experienced teachers need to organize the things they know into a coherent scheme. Call it a theory or philosophy. Obviously, we all need to learn new things as they become available.

For several years, I have been teaching a course called The Composition Process. It is designed primarily for teacher-preparation candidates, but many experienced teachers take it as well. At the end of the session, instead of an examination, I ask my students to write their own "philosophy of teaching composition" or possibly what they think may be an emerging philosophy, since many of them have not yet been in the classroom. It is always fascinating to read the essays, and I am particularly pleased when some of them tell me that they could not have written on the topic before they took the course, even though all of them have been involved in writing throughout their school careers, many of them have taken writing courses of various kinds, and some of them have actually taught writing. Not many English majors think seriously about the process and psychology of writing. They haven't been asked to. Writing a philosophy is an attempt to provide a center that will hold so that things do not fall apart.

I think I understand why many teachers, particularly high school teachers, approach the teaching of writing unenthusiastically. First of all, not many colleges provide adequate preparation for prospective teachers, despite the fact that school administrators have for years decried the imbalance in the preparation of English teachers. Again and again English majors enter teaching prepared only to teach literature. Once in the system, teaching composition becomes such a demanding daily job that few people have time to study, to read professional literature, to assess their own values, or to work out anything that might possibly correspond to a coherent philosophy. Characteristically, teachers follow the text. As a result, they become practitioners, not theorists—followers, not planners—and sometimes they fail to recognize that what they do on Thursday contradicts in theory what they did on Tuesday. Further, there are never-ending bundles of papers to read. But I don't have to document the busyness of English teachers or to expound upon the priorities many of them hold. The shoddiness of composition teaching is one of the unfortunate and harsh realities of the schools at all levels, but teachers must not be made to assume all of the blame. School systems have to share responsibility also. The public may call for better preparation in writing, but, if that is to occur, the schools and the public supporting the schools have to provide teachers with schedules and student loads that will give them the opportunity to do a good job when they try.

In this book I want to make a number of observations that I consider helpful in teaching writing or preparing to do it. I don't presume to say that it is *necessary* to know these things, but—to repeat—they may be helpful in giving a teacher confidence. I would not want to eliminate entirely the trial-and-error process of learning to teach well, but, in turn, I see no reason why each person has to hit every chuckhole along the way.

In writing about the teaching of writing, I intend at times, quite unapologetically, to be autobiographical and anecdotal, talking about my own experiences as a teacher and a director of Freshman English and about the experiences of some people with whom I have worked. I am no fledgling. Neither do I consider myself a sage who knows it all. I have learned much in thirty years about the teaching of writing. I would be sad to say that I had not. But of far greater importance is that I continue to learn. Because writing is always a product of individuals in a particular setting at a particular time in the context of prevailing values of that time, I find that I must constantly reexamine my approaches and, if necessary, alter my perceptions and conclusions about writing as time passes and conditions change. This is not a betrayal of old values. I look upon it as necessary flexibility to offset the claim of some people that writing is now obsolescent and dying. I think it need not be, but as a discipline it may very well be an endangered species.

I also continue to learn because more and more responsible work on writing and rhetoric is being published. Gary Tate's *Teaching Composition: Ten Bibliographical Essays* testifies to a growing number of serious works on the subject. Somewhat to my surprise, not many books on the teaching of writing exist—that is, on expository writing. I don't know exactly what the explanation is. Perhaps texts for students have been implicitly considered texts for teachers as well, and certainly there is no dearth of student texts. But I don't think a handbook or rhetoric addressed to students substitutes for a book on teaching addressed specifically to teachers, particularly if the book aims to help teachers find a compatible way of teaching, not to promote what the author thinks is one best way for everybody. As far as I am concerned, there is no *one* best way, but there are good ways and there are bad ways. The bad ways provide gimmicks and keep students wondering how to write better. The good ways help them become self-sufficient thinkers and writers, confident in their ability to produce and to view their own writing critically. The job is not simple, but it becomes simpler if we begin to understand the complexities we are dealing with. That's what this book is about.

Part I

THE PROCESS

1

Lore and Folklore About Writing

In 1947, after I had completed a master's degree, I transferred to a different university to work for a Ph.D. I needed money to continue my studies, but I knew little at that time about assistantships and scholarships. Two or three days after classes had begun, I made an appointment with the department chairman to find out if there was any job I could do in the department. He made a few inquiries: Yes, I had worked for a teaching certificate as an undergraduate. Yes, I had taught English and Social Science for about one and a half years in junior high school before and immediately after World War II. Did I want to teach one section of Freshman English? Indeed I did. There was still one section without an instructor. I could teach it if I wanted to.

That was my introduction to a college writing course. A handbook and a workbook. A few guidelines about the writing requirement and grading. Nothing else. No meetings. No specific instructions. No follow-up. No evaluation. I was completely on my own. This kind of introduction to writing, I understand, at both the secondary and college level, is not at all uncommon. No wonder writing is often poorly taught. Teachers are seldom prepared to do it and not asked whether they are prepared. The assumption seems to be that anyone can teach writing. We assume that anyone who can write can teach writing, but we seldom even know whether the teacher can write, at least write well. Surveys consistently indicate that English teachers have little confidence in their ability to teach writing. When they are catapulted into a job, they fall back desperately upon their own experience, good or bad. Or they may choose a favorite teacher in the past to emulate. They repeat what they at some time in the past have heard or read without thinking about the implications or consistency of their advice. Or, naturally, they enforce what the text may say without questioning its premises. As a result of these practices, there is a vast lore about writing—some of it folklore—and very little of it gets examined critically.

Upon occasion when I have had English teachers in class or those preparing to teach English, I ask them to list the ten most self-evident statements they can make about writing or the teaching of writing—things they believe, things they take for granted as truths, things they seldom say out loud because they seem so obvious. The list is instructive. It gets at what I call the lore and folklore about writing. Obviously, I cannot go through an entire list, but I would like to select a few of these statements and reflect briefly on their implications for the teaching of writing.

First, here are the self-evident statements that I consider for the most part true.

1. *In order to write, we have to put down one word before we write another word.*

The obviousness of this statement, espccially to anyone who types, clearly puts it in the category of things that we ordinarily don't say out loud. Why, then, should we think about it at all?

First, the actual transcription of words on paper gives writing a kind of built-in linearity. A thought has to be strung out word by word, although it may have flashed into our minds as an image, as a whole, as a concept. We control words in writing more tightly than we do in speaking. Writing is not actually thinking transcribed. It is thinking channeled into words or, as some say, it is a special kind of mental process, a mode of learning in itself.[1]

Second, the actual transcription of words on paper places special focus on grammatical order. If we had to make separate and conscious decisions about every sequence we wrote, we would be considerably handicapped. We don't, of course. We refer to an internalized system of grammar that we intuitively draw upon—thus, the usual advantage of native speakers over second-language learners. And the resulting awkwardness when even native speakers belabor too much the matter of order for special effect. Subject-verb-object/complement is the most natural pattern of the English language. When we tamper too much with it by inverting or interrupting it, we begin to upset the easy flow of words.

Further, as we think of the linearity of writing and speaking, we need to remind ourselves of another obvious fact: we perceive other arts differently. We experience painting and photography simultaneously. Film, dance, and music, although they depend upon certain linear elements in production, are also simultaneous in perception. But we must write and we must read linearly.

Several years ago when I gave a talk at NCTE on nonlinear logic, I was interrupted quite unexpectedly by a kind of spontaneous applause expressing combined surprise and approval by one teacher, who then, embarrassed by her enthusiasm, felt obliged to explain her interruption. She said I was the only person who in any way accounted for the difficulty she thought her students were having with traditional linear expression when most of the daily influences upon them, including TV, were nonlinear. In that talk, I had been conjecturing that those of us

---

[1] Janet Emig, "Writing as a Mode of Learning," *College Composition and Communication*, 28 (1977), 122-128.

whose intellectual perceptions have been shaped by a linear-verbal model might not yet be ready to recognize symptoms of cultural change, Marshall McLuhan notwithstanding. At another meeting not too long after that one, I heard a college professor say, "My students no longer seem to have a sense of structure." I responded that I found it difficult to believe that students of college age lacked a sense of structure. Perhaps they perceived structures differently. And that I think is a possibility to be considered in teaching any group of students who in their formative years have learned most of what they know not from linear books, but from multi-dimensional media. We should recognize that just the linear demands of writing terrify a good number of people. They are less terrified of talking because they think less about linear structure when they are doing it.

2. *Most people don't like to write.*

Basically, I think this is true. For a large number of that group, however, we have to qualify the statement. What many people don't like is to start writing. But if we can get them started, they often enjoy what they are doing and find some satisfaction in the finished product. Getting started is a major barrier—a mental block—usually overcome by the pressure of a deadline.

But why the reluctance about writing? First of all, I think many people believe they are being forced into an activity they don't know how to do and don't do very well. One student put the thought bluntly, "Writing lousy is very depressing." Furthermore, because most teachers don't come forth with ten easy steps toward better writing and don't seem able to explain why they can't, they perpetuate the mystery about writing and implicitly support the proposition that writing is a kind of inborn talent; you have it or you don't. Perhaps this book can help dispel the mystery by explaining the nature of writing and how best we can teach it.

Second, I think many people don't like to write because they are afraid to try, especially in a school setting. They want to avoid the negative comments they know are coming. We have to admit that teachers do not tolerate flaws in student writing in the way that they sometimes rationalize the flaws of professional writers. Obviously, as teachers, we have a special way of reading. That's another matter for further discussion: is the teacher of writing primarily an editor? I constantly remind myself of a sentence I once heard William Stafford include in a speech at a San Francisco meeting. I wrote it down at the time: "In matters of writing, we must forgive each other much." It's an inscription that ought to be engraved over every classroom door.

3. *By its nature, writing is a solitary experience.*

This fact may very well be seen as an explanation of No. 2, one of the reasons some people do not like to write. Writing is basically a private act, and a lonely one. Others can function as critics or proofreaders, but the source of the writing is the self. I have never seen a group of people successfully compose a joint statement. The solution is always to give it to one person to write a draft and submit it to the others for response. Any sentence someone substitutes for one of our own is that person's, not ours. Writing is a dynamic process involving choices. We cannot write as a computer does because we are not all programmed identically. Thus we produce differently. What we share is the grammar of the language, the basic meanings of words, and the conventions of mauscript form. Most of the other elements of arrangement and style are individual and variable. Thus, writing becomes an act that we must do on our own if we are to do it successfully. One of the big conflicts in the teaching of writing is the degree to which we can and should routinize the way people go about the act of writing.

4. *Writing is not as natural as speaking.*

I am not certain this is a fact as phrased, but it's the way the thought usually gets expressed. Let's admit that talking is easier than writing and that we are often more willing to talk than to write. Talking doesn't trap us into commitment as readily as writing. But, after we admit those tendencies, is there anything actually unnatural about writing? Or is writing something like a special dialect of speech? Or a far more controlled and developed form of speech? When a ballet dancer leaps high into the air, the performer is doing something we can all do to some degree. The dancer simply demonstrates a degree of skill—perhaps talent—that we have not developed. Being able to write is somewhat the same. We are all capable of verbalizing to some degree. The task of the schools is to extend the abilities of students to speak and write. Writing is frequently the more demanding form of verbalization. At that point, we tend to think of it as less natural.

5. *We learn writing best by doing it.*

Despite the obviousness of this statement, some teachers attempt to teach writing by eliminating writing. They substitute reading, drills, discussion, film and hope that proficiency in writing will follow. All of these classroom activities may very well help in the writing process, as we will see further on, but they cannot substitute for putting pen to paper. As complex as writing is when we consider the extent to which it involves the total self, we must not ignore the fact that it is, in part, a skill that will improve if it is practiced and if the writer keeps a critical eye on the final product. Success in writing demands more than one try, but we of course have to agree what success in writing means. Some teachers define success in terms of gaining self-confidence, others in terms of correctness or expressiveness or flexibility or appropriateness or effectiveness. These are not exclusive of one another. They overlap, but they are different objectives and may well require different approaches in teaching.

.   .   .

When I ask students for lore about writing, they inevitably give me folklore as well. Folklore includes the myths. Some of these statements are die-hard falsities that get repeated over and over. Others are controversial; that is, we may simply not know whether they are true or false, but we act as if we know and proceed accordingly. I would like to examine a few of these and their implications.

1. *Anyone who can talk, can write.*

Anyone who has taught a composition course knows that this statement is a myth. Repeatedly, I am impressed by the fluency and sophistication of seventeen-and eighteen-year-olds when they talk, but when they are asked to write, many of them are initially paralyzed and only strugglingly force out a few words. The results are self-conscious, labored, and dull. Why does this happen? The first reason we have already discussed briefly in referring to the fear and paranoia that grip many people as they approach writing. A second reason is that we can be impressive if we have to talk for only 30 or 45 seconds. Writing is a sustained effort, requiring contemplation and control. Further, readers can subject prose to close scrutiny. True, both talking and writing are forms of verbalization, but the loosely structured sentences and excess verbiage that pass for conversation or discussion do not translate well into writing. A test is to see in written form something we have spoken extemporaneously. Several years ago, I was invited to participate in a panel at a state educational meeting. Several questions were posed. Then, each panelist was invited to talk five or ten minutes. I was not aware that the session was being taped.

A month or two later, I received a transcription of my remarks because plans were being made to publish the results of the discussion. I was asked if I wished to edit my comments. After I read them, I was satisfied with the substance of the remarks, but I found it necessary to go through the copy and simply strike out words that served as fillers while I was apparently thinking ahead to the next thing I was going to say. Although the result was a tightened, readable comment, I do not think the edited version would have served as well for the original speaking occasion. Talking and writing require different styles.

Although we should recognize the differences between talking and writing, we should not think of talk as working at cross-purposes with writing. Talking often emerges in easy rhythms. The test of many a sentence is to read it aloud to see how it sounds. Also, talking is often more productive of ideas than writing. We can actually generate more ideas by talking for a set time than we can by writing for the same length of time. One of the main reasons is that we do not tolerate silence easily. We force ourselves to think and speak without too much prior censorship or editing. Writing is slower because the transcription is slower, but also because we often think too hard upon the thought.

2. *Writing can't be taught.*

How can teachers teach writing if it can't be taught? The answer is simple. They can act as if they are teaching writing. They can ask for writing and read it and then fill in class time teaching any number of other things that they consider teachable. I am reminded of Francis Christensen's comment: "In composition courses we do not really teach our captive charges to write better—we merely *expect* them to. And we do not teach them how to write better because we do not know how to teach them to write better. And so we merely go through the motions."[2]

Teaching anything ought to be based on the belief that it can be taught. I am convinced that many people repeat this particular myth because they themselves don't know how to teach writing and furthermore don't really want to know because they find the job burdensome and frustrating. In brief, saying writing can't be taught is a cop-out. This book says it can be taught.

There is another myth related to the one above. Those who repeat it do not categorically say writing can't be taught, but they say we don't actually know what we are doing. What these nay-sayers mean is that we don't know *with certainty* what we are doing; we do not know with scientific precision, with verifiable data, or with testproof accuracy. Of course, we don't. But much of what we do, however diverse, is intuitively sound, and experience confirms it. We will never be able to teach writing with the precision of laboratory technicians, but we can proceed at least with the kind of self-confidence that experienced and knowledgeable gardeners have, who combine facts with ob-

---

[2]"A Generative Rhetoric of the Sentence" in *The Sentence and the Paragraph* (Champaign, Ill.: NCTE, 1966), p. 1.

servation and a good bit of hope, especially to meet those variables, like the weather, that are not within their control. Gardeners go about their work with expectation and flexibility. Teachers ought to do the same, recognizing that they can no more teach students to grow than gardeners can teach plants. They can, however, like gardeners, provide the necessary conditions for growth.

3. *A writing course should begin with basics.*

This is another myth that teachers repeat because of their continuing belief that most students come to them inadequately prepared. It applies to almost any level. What it also does is to justify the so-called *need* for review. As a result, course after course begins at zero, namely, with the noun, and writing gets deferred again.

We can change myth to sound principle very simply if we say: a writing course should always begin with writing. Then, and only then, will a teacher be able to determine whether those students are unprepared. Then, and only then, will a teacher be able to ascertain what the general needs of a class are and decide what to emphasize. "Review" is another evasion of the hard job of helping students develop their writing ability.

4. *Writing should not be forced on students.*

Much depends in this statement upon the meaning of "forced." Obviously, writing should never be used as a penalty. A good many writing assignments are given in the spirit of punishment. As a result, students begin to attach unpleasant associations to writing.

If writing were completely voluntary, especially in an academic setting, how many students would choose to write? Several years ago an overly idealistic teaching assistant in my department told his students that they had the option of choosing their mode of expression. If they wanted to paint pictures, they could. If they wanted to tape thoughts, they could. If they wanted to write songs, they could. When I took over his class shortly after his termination (a writing course is not a course in painting), I learned that only five of twenty-five students had opted to write.

Should students be required to write? By all means if writing is important enough to be taught. And I see nothing unrealistic or purely academic about writing upon assignment. I think most writing is done as some form of assignment, whether it is a freelance writer finishing a story for a magazine, a householder writing a letter of complaint to the telephone company, a professor writing to avoid perishing, or one friend responding to the letter of another friend. We need only ask ourselves when we last wrote on a completely voluntary basis.

5. *There is no connection between the teaching of grammar and improvement in student writing.*

I include this statement in the folkore because it is clearly open to challenge, despite a number of research studies that support the statement. Great numbers of teachers still claim there *is* a connection, and there are research studies that support that view; for example, a project such as the Bateman-Zidonis study of 1964 indicates that students instructed in transformational grammar improved significantly over those students who did not have similar instruction.[3] In a recent article, Janice Neuleib, reviewing several of the research studies that pre-date the new grammars, focuses on the limitations of those studies and their tendency to make sweeping conclusions on the basis of one experiment. She stresses the need for reinvestigation, duplication of studies, and continuing evaluation.[4] The relation of grammar and writing is one of the enduring controversies of English studies, and I don't think the dissension is likely to die—or be resolved by my remarks.

I'm not going to attempt a rational argument on the subject, only a personal testimonial. I have found the grammatical knowledge I have acquired immensely useful to me as a writer,

---

[3]D. R. Bateman and F. J. Zidonis, *The Effect of a Study of Transformational Grammar on the Writing of Ninth and Tenth Graders* (Champaign, Ill.: NCTE Research Report No. 6, 1966).

[4]"The Relation of Formal Grammar to Composition," *College Composition and Communication*, 28 (1977), 247–250. See also Elaine Chaika, "Grammars and Teaching," *College English*, 39 (1978), 770–783.

and I often wish I had more. I constantly use grammatical facts to avoid errors and gaucheries. I know I am more conscious of stylistic effects by being aware of structures. And, of course, as a teacher I have found grammar invaluable in diagnosing writing problems and explaining them to others. Having said these things, I am also fully aware that the refutation by the unbeliever can be brief; it can read simply: "I get along without grammar very well." And that is also undoubtedly true. Thus the controversy continues.

In making a defense of grammatical study in English classes, particularly in grades 7, 8, and 9, I would like to add a caveat. I do not mean to confuse the teaching of grammar with the teaching of writing. The two are not the same, but they can be brought to bear upon one another. Grammarians are not necessarily writers, but writers must always be grammarians, whether they are conscious of what they are doing or not. In my own case, I like to know what I am doing.

Why Teach Writing Anyway?

In the 1960s, as part of a program following an institute for English teachers at the University of Washington, I visited thirty-five high schools in the immediate area. My purpose was to assess whether the institute had had any noticeable effect on the teachers who had attended. I sat in on English classes at each school and then talked informally with the teachers. In one school, I asked one teacher what kind of writing instruction she was giving. It was then that I got a response something like the following: "I'll confess to you, Dr. Irmscher, I don't do very much with writing. I've never been able to convince myself that putting in all that time on papers is really worthwhile. Most of these students aren't going to college, and for the rest of their lives most of them will never do more than write a few letters to their parents or friends. I think I can spend my time and effort doing something more worthwhile."

I think about that comment with a kind of sadness, not because it revealed a condition I was unaware of, but because it told me that a teacher who had already taught English for more than twenty years could not justify the teaching of writing on anything but a utilitarian basis: students wouldn't use the skill, as if we were teaching them to ski where there was no snow. A useless activity.

Perhaps we should all face the hard fact that if we have to justify the teaching of writing to parents or colleagues or school boards on practical needs alone, then we are going to have a tough case. Great numbers of people, high school and college graduates alike, do not often have to write anything of importance. And if they have to communicate a message, they have telephones and tapes and secretaries and all the as-yet-uninvented electronic media that can serve as surrogates. Writing is not necessarily the most efficient form of communication for messages. Even students who go to college can manage by a careful selection of their courses to get through four years without writing a paper. All of us can survive without writing. In fact, in our society, we can even succeed, if success is measured in dollars and cents, not in thoughts and words.

But is writing no longer necessary? If we shift our thinking away from what writing does for others—a means of communication—to what writing does for us as individuals—a means of self-realization and self-knowledge—then writing may be even *more* necessary. I don't know anyone who asks "Why think anyway?" or "Why talk anyway?" or "Why communicate anyway?" If we basically consider ourselves social beings, we consider these natural, spontaneous forms of human behavior. They are necessary functions of our being. But we also have to remind ourselves that we do not learn them under the specialized instruction of the school. Writing is different in the sense that we acquire the skill as a learned experience in a school setting. Yet writing does for the individual what thinking, talking, and communicating do and does it in a unique way. What is its special character?

Perhaps the fact that writing is a less spontaneous act than thinking, talking, or communicating by other means gives it a peculiar advantage. In *The Art of Loving*, Erich Fromm laments the modern person's inability, even refusal, to concentrate. We constantly divert ourselves; we often do two things at once: eat and listen to music, look at TV and knit, or talk and smoke. Writing is a way of counteracting our distractedness. It requires concentration, focus, and discipline, usually in a silent and solitary setting. Because writing is so much more deliberative than talking, it helps us determine what we know and what we don't know. In our minds, we can fool ourselves. Not on paper. If no thought is in our minds, nothing comes out. Mental fuzziness translates into words only as fuzziness or meaninglessness.

Writing is often thinking about our own thoughts; that is, it permits us to distance ourselves from our own thoughts, to separate the thought from the thinker—a kind of analyzing and assessing, a resolving of differences, and a final structuring. Perhaps most important of all, writing permits us not just to say what we have to say, but to *see* what we have to say. Thus we have a new concern for the *how* as well as the *what*, the manner as well as the substance.

Because the way something is expressed in writing is consistently important, writing increases the need for choices. We need more words to select from, more combinations, more structures, more strategies. Writing is a greater challenge to the imagination than talking. Writing requires a mature ability to use language. It can act as a positive influence upon the creative powers of the individual. In fact, many people first discover their full capacities for expression by meeting the challenges of writing.

Jacques Barzun reminds us that writing often begins with an intent, not a finished thought. The act of writing is a generative process. We discover as we write. Writing stimulates thinking, chiefly because it forces us to concentrate and organize. Talking does, too, but writing allows more time for introspection and deliberation.

What I am referring to in these paragraphs is a kind of practical value to the individual that goes beyond simple communication. Writing may be important, not because it allows a student to write examinations in the classroom, but because it demands the kind of thinking and preparation that are preliminary to being able to write. In some cases, writing is an intellectual discipline; in others, it is an emotional catharsis. In either case, the value is personal—something that we do to help ourselves, not others. The intrinsic values of writing should prompt us not to repeat "Why write anyway?" but "Why not?" Why limit ourselves to other media? Why discard a resource of proven value for self-expression, self-understanding, and self-discipline—a means of expression that prompted Robert B. Heilman to write: "Many of us have experienced the sense of being put together by the process of putting together. We have composed, and in a sense we are composed."[1]

The kinds of personal reasons I have been stressing are difficult to articulate persuasively to others because we have to learn them from our own experience. That's why teachers of writing should know what writing entails—both the frustrations and the pleasures—before they attempt to teach others. Yet we often have nonperforming teachers of writing. Consequently, they are unaware of the possibilities of writing. They are ignorant of the consequences of any given writing assignment. I recall one instructor who in class always wrote on one of the topics he gave his own students. And, like everyone else, he submitted his own work to open criticism by the class. The nonwriting teacher of composition often can say only what is wrong with writing, forgetting how important—in fact, how crucial—encouragement and support are to the writer. Both teachers and students need to be convinced of the value of what they are doing. If they aren't, then the motivation is lacking, and writing will be simply another school exercise done because it is demanded.

---

[1] "Except He Come to Composition," *College Composition and Communication*, 21 (1970), 232.

3

What Do We Do When We Teach Writing?

If we ask what we do when we teach literature or language, we get fairly explicit answers. We may discuss literary movements or history or biography or criticism. We may convey knowledge or create understanding or develop appreciation. But what do we do when we teach writing? Do we concentrate on the effects of writing—a course in persuasion or varieties of prose style? Do we teach what Robert Graves once called "success English," the purpose of which is "to make a bad cause seem better by a skillful hypnotic arrangement of words"? Do we prepare students to think analytically? Do we focus on process—how to go about the job? Or do we look only at the results—the written essay—so that our chief function is editing? What do we do when we teach writing, or better yet, what *should* we do to help students develop their writing abilities?

First, we ought to confront one hard fact: good writers do not have to be taught; they can be completely self-taught. Natural talent alone does not explain their accomplishment. Self-development does. But what have they done as a substitute for formal instruction? The simplest answer is that they have of their own accord developed the staples of the writer: a respect for language, an ear for sound, a taste for phrase, and a sense of proportion. And they have done it primarily through their own reading. Reading is ultimately the best teacher of writing. The difference between the self-taught, talented writers and struggling writers is the degree to which their intuitive resources are developed. Talented writers trust their intuitions because they have a sense of their rightness. Strugglers lack that confidence. They want prescriptions that will solve their difficulties; they seek solutions outside themselves rather than within themselves. No wonder they continue to struggle.

If we use textbooks as a guide, we can say without too great risk that the emphasis in the teaching of writing up until the 1960s was primarily on the product—the final written essay. That is, the teacher issued the command "Write." The students wrote, turned in their essays, and at that point the teaching of writing supposedly began. Correction. Comment. Revision. Repeat performance.

Some of the texts, of course, had sections on "Choosing a Subject" and "Narrowing the Topic," but essentially what went on before the paper was turned in was the writer's business. Most of us would agree that what occurs before the first written draft is highly important, yet most teachers in the past thought that the act of composing was not their concern, only the product.

Now, more and more theorists are saying that if we are going to help students become better writers we will have to help them when they most need help. That doesn't mean sitting next to them to question and guide them, but it does mean giving them resources they can use to generate and shape ideas. No easy task, for with this changed emphasis we concern ourselves with the behavior of human beings in the act of writing as well as with the sentences they write. The new concern with Process, as opposed to Product, requires us to rethink the basic definition of writing. Is it a skill, as we have been calling it up to this point? If so, what approaches are appropriate to the teaching of skills? Is writing an art? If so, is an art taught differently from a skill? Or is writing an even more inclusive mode of behavior? If so, how will that broader concept affect teaching?

Skills, like the word *creativity*, conjures up a whole range of meanings and connotations, both good and bad. I would therefore like to separate some of those meanings and arrange them in a hierarchy. In doing this, I am drawing heavily upon a monograph by Irving A. Taylor called "The Nature of the Creative Process."[1] Taylor found that people could seldom talk intelligently about creativity because they consistently attached different meanings to the word. He therefore collected about 100 definitions of creativity and categorized them as follows:

1. Expressive creativity
2. Productive creativity
3. Inventive creativity
4. Innovative creativity
5. Emergentive creativity

Because the differences among these five levels are sufficiently important if we are to understand what occurs in writing, I want to explain Taylor's terms briefly and apply them in my own way to writing.

In Taylor's first stage, expressive creativity, the chief aim is self-expression. In the spontaneous drawings of children, skills are unimportant, just as skills have little importance when we doodle. Representationalism is not a special value any more than proportion, aptness, or correctness. But exploration and spontaneity are. They are also important in certain kinds of expressive writing, in meditations and diary entries and journals. In such forms, fluency is more important than control. One of the chief aims is uninhibited expression.

In the second stage, productive creativity, Taylor stresses that skills need to be acquired to produce finished, recognizable

---

[1]In *Creativity: An Examination of the Creative Process. A Report on the Third Communications Conference of the Art Directors Club of New York,* ed. Paul Smith (New York: Hastings House, 1959), pp. 51–82.

objects. In drawing, realism becomes a new aim; cats should look like cats and houses should look like houses. Developing skills further depends upon mastery and control. In writing, this stage is represented by basic utilitarian prose. Its chief virtues are clarity, coherence, and correctness. The message must come through simply and clearly.

Taylor's third stage, inventive creativity, depends strongly on a mastery of the productive skills. Having mastered those, the individual can discover ways to use them flexibly and individually, to see old things in new ways, perceive new relationships, and put the imprint of ingenuity upon them. At this stage, writers develop a confidence with language that lets them control words, not the other way around. As a result, they develop an identifiable style. Effectiveness becomes a concern beyond simple efficiency.

The final two stages Taylor discusses are higher forms of creativity and therefore rarely achieved. He defines innovative creativity as the stage in which the individual sufficiently understands the assumptions of an art or science so as to modify its course in some way. In prose, we might think of Bacon or Hemingway or, in poetry, of Donne or Stevens. Emergentive creativity exists only at the most abstract level, resulting in an entirely new principle or assumption that alters completely our way of organizing experience. Hence we must turn to special geniuses like Einstein, Curie, Freud, Picasso, Stravinsky, and Joyce.

Taylor's categories let us explain a good bit of confusion about the teaching of writing. First of all, we can separate the geniuses of Levels 4 and 5 from fairly ordinary, intelligent people who are capable of moving through the first three levels. As teachers, we should be sensitive to signs of special talent, but, at the same time, we should not mistake rampant expressiveness for true innovative power. A good bit of Level-1 creativity at times passes for Level-4 creativity until we recognize the distinction between eccentricity and originality.

These levels may also help us explain why a good number of students never reach the flexibility and confidence characteristic of Level 3. If they have failed to gain proficiency in the productive skills of language, then it is not likely that they will be capable of artistry except by accident. In the performing arts, including athletics, we know that basic preparation comes first, followed by practice for proficiency, followed by inventiveness and varying degrees of artistry depending upon the creative capacity of the individual and the amount of time and energy the individual wants to expend. Artistry emerges, but it depends upon a development of skills. If we think of writing also as a performing art, the rest should follow.

One of the characteristic things about learning the skills of many activities is that the professionals usually have a "best" way to recommend. If we were able to learn to write the way we learn to hit a golf ball, play scales on the piano, or bevel a piece of wood, then all we would have to do is to decide which way was best and teach it. But we know that writing involves more than learning a grip or manipulating the fingers or determining the grain of wood. The irony is that English experts don't often agree on the best way to teach what are considered basic skills: spelling, verb forms, agreement of subject and verb, the dangling modifier, and so on. And some do not even consider them necessary at all because these teachers are less interested in the social conventions of writing or in artistry than they are in self-expression. To them, skills are not essential. In fact, they are considered stifling.[2] Since language is a means of self-identity, writing becomes a way of finding one's identity. To them, the chief values in writing are sincerity and openness.

Each of the definitions we have dealt with—writing as a skill, writing as an art, and writing as self-expression—has its

---

[2]Here is an exact quotation from a prospective teacher: "Often instructors tend to focus specifically on the mechanics of writing rather than the development of individual style and technique. That is why many writers have a tendency to write in a manner that neglects or denies the fundamentals when they are no longer confronted with the classroom situation. Mechanics, such as spelling and punctuation, have become so monotonous and stifling to individual style that the student of writing seems to have a subconscious desire to rid himself of such 'unpleasantries' once outside the educational system." Whether or not one accepts this point of view, it is important to note that some of the things we do as teachers, intending to help, become counter-productive.

advocates, and they often dispute with one another as if their aims conflicted. We would not have to hunt long to find teachers who would claim that emphasis on basic skills inhibits creativity or to find teachers who would draw a clear line of distinction between expository and creative writing and exclude any kind of creative exercise from the classroom. To such extremists, writing would appear to be either an expression of feeling or an expression of thought. Freedom becomes the keyword of educational romantics; discipline, the keyword of educational classicists—a somewhat less appropriate label for them, but one that identifies those who represent orderliness, convention (often synonymous with correctness), and practicality in writing as opposed to those who promote spontaneity, individuality, and imaginativeness.

Every ten or twenty years, a major change of emphasis occurs, depending upon war, taxes, and the prevailing morality. It is tempting to think of the shift from romanticism to classicism and then back to neo-romanticism and to neo-classicism again as a pendulum-like movement. But the metaphor is far too regular and mechanical to reflect what goes on at any particular time. Changes in education are much more wave-like. They come in with different surges, some big, some small. And there is always the undertow, something pulling powerfully in the opposite direction. Anybody who wades in feels both movements simultaneously. This, it seems to me, is the dilemma of the teacher of writing, particularly the new teacher. How does that person keep from being swirled about by conflicting currents?

Having worked with teaching assistants for a great number of years, I can say that the single most important thing each of them has to learn is what concessions to make to freedom and what concessions to make to discipline, depending upon their individual temperaments. We first have to recognize in which direction we tend as personalities and then attempt to compensate. At their best, disciplinarians as teachers are challenging, thorough, and methodical; at their worst, they are sterile, rigid, and purposelessly demanding. At their best, romantics as teachers are inspiring, understanding, and flexible; at their worst, they are slack, solipsistic, and erratic. What is best and worst is determined by their effect upon students—in brief, whether they help students develop their ability to write, not in fluency alone, but in control as well.

Is there another way of thinking about the teaching of writing that makes the teacher more than a skills technician or an amateur therapist?

In considering the nature of the composition process and the way to teach it, I am convinced that the difficulty lies not in the truth or falsity of various definitions we have considered, but in the limitations of each to describe fully what is involved. True, writing is in part skill. Parts of it can—and should—be mastered as skills; they are ordinarily mastered by imitation and repeated practice. True, writing can also be an art, although artistry does not consistently develop, as Taylor suggests, from simple to complex. The untutored can prematurely produce remarkably mature and effective work. And it is true that writing is also self-expression, although it becomes less and less so to the extent that the individual negates an identifiable voice to produce an encyclopedic kind of prose that we refer to familiarly as the Plain Style.

The basic premise of this book is that writing is a complex form of behavior. It is a way of acting with language that involves the total being—our thoughts and feelings and attitudes and tastes and verbal resources. Writing can be highly conventional or uniquely personal, just as individuals tend to be. Some kinds of writing may be routine, almost mechanically done. Other kinds may be markedly inventive and original. We do not write alike anymore than we talk alike, and we do not write the same on all occasions. Is there, then, anything teachable about such a highly individualized form of behavior?

What we can teach in writing is what we share when we engage in this form of behavior. We think, we feel, we shape thoughts and emotions, we verbalize, we seek effects, we transcribe. These are the six components of writing to which we will give attention in this book: ideas, emotions, structures, words, styles, and mechanics.

Concerning these components, we can observe patterns of behavior and make generalizations, but there are few rules about how to compose. Attempts to codify the process—to reduce it to steps and imperatives—are attempts to make teaching easy, but they deny the fundamental concept of writing as behavior. Should we write lock step the way we march? It is easy to say, "Always prepare a formal outline before you begin to write," as if that insures an organized paper, but planning and making a formal outline are not necessarily one and the same. They may be for some people, but certainly not all. Insisting upon a formal outline in advance denies the fundamental and important notion of writing as discovery. Call it adaptive behavior. By insisting upon uniform behavior, we can run counter to what may be an individual's strongest and best inclinations.

When we think of writing as a skill, we emphasize craftsmanship, doing accurately and well what we write. When we think of writing as an art, we emphasize style, the mark of artistry with which the job can be accomplished. But we need not limit artistry to belletristic writing. Style may well be an important variable in work-a-day writing, including reports, reviews, and memoranda. When we think of writing as self-expression, we emphasize individuality, the uniqueness of experience and the revelation of feeling. When we think of writing as a form of behavior, we emphasize the psychology of the total act from beginning to end. Writing is overcoming inhibitions. Writing is getting started. Writing is opening up. Writing is controlling. Writing is matching words to thoughts. Writing is feeling as well as thinking. The process is actually a series of spontaneous acts involving choices and commitments more than it is a continuous, deliberative act. There are mental bursts, starts, and stops. What may be finally transcribed with order and effect is only a selected and edited version of the total generative process. In fact, the finished essay is only an illusion of what composing actually is.

In these terms, the teaching of writing concerned with process—with writing as behavior—becomes far more than reading papers and editing them. Teaching becomes a way of eliciting the most desirable behavior from each individual as a writer. That is dependent upon some understanding of the role that intuition plays in composition.

4

Acknowledging Intuition

If we think of ourselves as writers, we know that the several hours we allot to writing a paper do not adequately account for all of the thought, anxiety, involvement, perhaps excitement, that have gone into its preparation. Mulling over a project can be productive, not because it leads anywhere immediately, but because it sets into motion a subconscious or pre-conscious activity that has a way of operating without our awareness of it. The result is often an idea or hunch or grasp that comes as an illumination—nothing necessarily revelatory, but an insight that comes with such suddenness that we are tempted to think of it as a reward for our obsessiveness. Intuition works that way.

We have all had the experience, I'm sure, of worrying a paper to a point of stagnation, only to abandon it in desperation and then find that the conscious mind has allowed the subconscious to solve the problem. The major limitation of this remarkable subconscious mechanism is that we seem not to be able to control it or to make it function when we think we need it most. As a result, we tend to be skeptical of intuition. We are

uncertain of its exact functioning. We fail to agree on a definition of it. Yet scientists, philosophers, psychologists, and artists
recognize intuition as a form of intelligent behavior. It plays an
important and continuing role in the writing process, especially
as a source of invention.

What most of us recognize as the intuitive leap or intuitive
grasp occurs in the pre-writing, preparatory stage. It is the break-
through; it produces the thought we need to start. But we do
not consistently depend upon intuition in this pre-operational
stage. It is an unexplainable heuristic. We are grateful when it
occurs, but we do not rely on it.

Once we begin writing, however, we are constantly dependent upon intuition for the choices we make. Grammatical
structure is primarily intuitional. I would advance that paragraphing is too. The kinds of choices we make about words,
arrangement, and style are not rational choices in the same
sense that we apply reason to evidence and argument. Composing is a process that calls constantly for spontaneous decisions—
where a sentence is heading, where it has ended, where emphasis
has or has not occurred, where the pace lags, where it would be
better to scratch out and start over. These are intuitive decisions. They indicate that intuition has a way of acting in habitual ways as well as in more striking moments of discovery.[1]

Looking at the revised manuscript of a well-known author—or even one of our own—gives us no idea of the constant
decision-making that occurs as we write. Any changes we see
were probably meditated upon, but the manuscript gives us no
notion whatsoever of the infinite number of other decisions and
rejections and alterations that never reach paper. Writing is of
necessity intuitively directed; it would be impossible to act without intuition. This fact is so much taken for granted or so often
ignored that it is seldom mentioned in texts on writing. It also
explains why some individuals have little or no need for instruc-

---

[1] In *The Mind Field* (New York: Grossman Publishers, 1976), Robert E. Ornstein
identifies the functioning of intuition primarily as right-brain activity. He notes, however, that any particular act may not exclusively involve right or left, but a blend,
drawing simultaneously on both components. One hemisphere may even serve as a
"backup" for the other. Writing seems to incorporate the blend of "sequence and
simultaneity" that he speaks of (pp. 32–34).

tion. Their intuitive resources are equal to the tasks they set for themselves.

Intuition is a kind of built-in teacher. For this reason, some teachers by profession don't want to talk about it at all for fear that they will no longer have a role. Others don't know what to say. More numerous are those who want to use intuition as an excuse for doing nothing at all; after all, one can't give someone else intuitions. All of these positions are based on a misunderstanding of what intuition is and how it functions.

Since we often trivialize the word *intuition* when we use it in a phrase like "blind intuition," we are entitled to ask if intuition has legitimate status among specialists, if it is a mental faculty seriously recognized or if it is only a word we popularly use to cover our ignorance of what we cannot otherwise explain. To be sure, many things remain unexplained about intuition, but it is an accepted human phenomenon, taken into account by theorists from Bergson to Bruner.[2] Our purpose here is not to review the literature on the subject, but to identify those characteristics of intuitive perception that pertain to writing.

Consider two general definitions. E. Fischbein defines the term as follows: "An intuition is a stabilised action programme which is derived from experience, and which is effective because of its global, immediate, and flexible qualities."[3] Richard Guggenheimer describes the intuitive mind as a "rich fabric of subconscious wisdom. By subconscious wisdom," he goes on to say, "I mean chains of logically bound and evaluated perceptions stored in memory."[4] Both definitions suggest a storing or programming of selected and related perceptions drawn from experience, applicable to new situations.

What is important to emphasize here is that intuition and instinct are not one and the same. Intuition must be educated. The more we have experienced, read, and reflected, the more likely we are to have spontaneous and sound intuitions in new

---

[2] Ornstein (p. 24) writes, "Although the phrase [intuition] is often maligned, conventionally used to indicate random guesswork or a mysterious combination of elements, it should be properly understood as *knowledge without recourse to inference.*"

[3] *The Intuitive Sources of Probabilistic Thinking in Children* (Boston: D. Reidel Publishing Co., 1975), p. 20.

[4] *Creative Vision in Artist and Audience* (New York: Harper, n.d.), p. 145.

situations. Intuition derives from both living experiences and experiences with language. Ben Shahn makes the point succinctly: "Intuition in art is actually the result of prolonged tuition."[5] Intuition begins with our responses to isolated incidents in experience and results in a cumulative and synthesized attitude or set of principles, internalized and structured, ready to affect future experience. It is a kind of personal progamming. Since it is strongly dependent upon observation and reading, those who are sensitive to things about them, who see more and see better, who read widely, are more likely to develop strong intuitions.

Intuition has a quality of immediacy; that is, it intervenes in moments of complexity to free us from the contradictions of rational thought. In this sense, it is one of the most practical and efficient resources we have, both inventively and habitually, for we can act with a "feeling" that we have chosen rightly. The "feeling" has nothing to do with physical sensation, but rather with intuitive conviction. We ordinarily use the words "I feel" or "I believe" to suggest the interaction of thought and feeling that induces us to act. We never say or even write "I intuit that . . . ." Yet we have acted on the basis of intuition.

We can now apply several of these points to the teaching of writing:

1. If intuitions represent perceptions we accumulate, internalize, and synthesize into patterns, we should then expect those individuals with limited experience in language, either in speaking, writing, listening, or reading, to have limited intuitions about language and less spontaneity in being able to write because they lack conviction in the immediate decision-making process that writing represents. Struggling writers do not trust the faint intuitions they have. Many of them are afraid because they are insecure. They want answers in terms of rules and prescriptions, but these characteristically lack the "global, immediate, and flexible qualities" that Fischbein speaks of.

2. Intuitions can be developed, strengthened, and changed, depending upon the experience and responsiveness of

---

[5] *The Shape of Content* (Cambridge: Harvard University Press, 1959), p. 108.

the individual. Repetitions add to the coherence, stability, and efficiency of our intuitive resources, but they cannot be crammed in like the study of facts for a test. Thus, the importance of continued practice in writing.

3. Our intuitive conviction—our intuitive sense of rightness—is closely related to our aesthetic sense of values, for the synthesis that intuition represents is based upon a selection and evaluation of perceptions. Our values may be subjective, but they are not unfounded; they are related to what we know and feel about past experiences. Intuitions help to apply established values to new situations. Conflicting intuitions signal the need to do more, to examine further, and, in some cases, to solve a dilemma by reference to logic.

4. Becoming a more mature writer means essentially transcending skills by developing intuitions. Amateur writers depend upon prescriptions and rules for guidelines that mature writers sense intuitively. Teachers who attempt to reduce the process of writing to a science fail to recognize that intuitions are able to guide writers flexibly and efficiently. The emphasis in science and the arts seems to vary. Applied science, although recognizing intuition, may often attempt to eliminate it as an unverifiable factor, whereas the arts seek to nourish it as a continuing source of creativity.

As we speak of intuition as a factor in writing, we should also anticipate a few common misunderstandings.

1. Saying intuitions should be developed and trusted is not the same as saying "do what comes naturally." One of the handicaps of remedial students is that their *natural* intuitions about language and writing often mislead them because they have not developed the patterns characteristic of the standard code of written English. If repetition reinforces principles and values that intuition draws upon, then we can see why many students have major difficulties overcoming the limitations of their home backgrounds, reading, and school training. They have not been subject to a gradual accumulation of intuitive resources that will allow them to be confident writers. We also have an explanation in part of why most remedial courses fail to have a noticeable effect upon students. Such courses address

surface features of writing that are not the major part of the problem.[6]

2. Recognizing that most of the choices about arrangement and style in writing are intuitive does not mean that these choices should be left untested. Revision is often a process of getting beyond the immediate decision to view a word or sentence or passage in a larger context. A slightly different perspective, especially someone else's, alters our way of responding. Intuitions are in no sense infallible. The teacher's role as reader-critic is important. Yet many teachers recognize that there is such a thing as discouraging the intuitive impulses of students by too much criticism, just as many writers recognize that there is such a thing as killing a work by too strenuous revision, that is, by deadening all that was fresh and intuitively spontaneous about a first choice.

3. Saying that writing depends constantly upon intuitive choices does not limit the number of good writers to a talented few. On the contrary, it expands the number possible. Intuition is a normal mental faculty common to all human beings, obviously more developed in some than in others, but capable of being strengthened in all.[7]

4. We know that intuitions can be formed without systematic instruction. The question arises whether systematic instruction can help. For the most part, teachers have given little attention to developing intuitions, or they have assumed that whatever goes on in the English classroom ought to help, often oblivious that some of the things they do are counter-intuitive. Oblique techniques—learning by indirection—are essential, especially in the teaching of writing. I believe in them. Yet many of our indirect techniques fail because students fail to see their

---

[6]Note Ornstein's observation (p. 40): "Because we do not conventionally educate, perceive, or credit a holistic, intuitive mode of knowledge, we find that reductions, substitutes, and palliatives are elevated beyond their nominal functions."

[7]Ornstein (p. 31) is emphatic on this point: "Intuition is not an obscure, mysterious function possessed by only a very few highly creative and unusual artists or scientists who produce interesting theories. Intuition is a faculty considered largely negative—creativity is romanticized, made external, considered unavailable to most ordinary people. The faculty of intuition is, rather, latent in all of us, a primary aspect of our cognitive abilities which we have allowed to degenerate."

purpose. In a survey we give to writing students at the University of Washington, we ask them if they think the reading in the course—sometimes selections of fiction, drama, and poetry—helped to make their writing better. At least one-half say "no," and their answers may be quite accurate. But there is also the possibility that many of them do not recognize what has occurred in the learning process. To them, indirection clearly means no direction. One of the reasons for uncertainty about teaching composition, particularly if we want to place new emphasis upon intuition as an active part of the process, is that we don't even have names for the kinds of intuitive resources we are talking about here. In an attempt to supply a direction and focus for these efforts, I would like to propose a working vocabulary of four terms. They are not intended to be an exhaustive set of terms, but they are a start. I have identified each of them as a "sense"—an intuitive sense—individually acquired, but with a sufficient range of similarity in most individuals in our society that we can think of them as norms. They are cultural norms, for they are derived from our perception of the things about us. These norms will vary with time. They will change when enough people perceive with a different sense of values.

The first "sense" I would like to identify is our sense of the "normative." I use it to refer primarily to matters of tone in writing. Just as our ears tolerate a range of sound comfortably—neither too soft nor too loud—so also our intuitive sense of the normative has limits as well. In an article entitled "Up Against the Wall, Mother! The Rhetoric of Slogans, Catchphrases, and Graffiti," Frank D'Angelo quotes Mark Rudd writing about the strike at Columbia University in 1968: "Perhaps nothing upset our enemies more than this slogan. To them it seemed to show the extent to which we had broken with their norms, how far we had sunk to brutality, hatred, and obscenity."[8]

If we want to define what Rudd means by "their norms," we would certainly have to include the restrained use of lan-

---

[8]*A Symposium in Rhetoric*, ed. W. E. Tanner, J. D. Bishop, and T. S. Kobler (Denton, Texas: Committee for the Federation Degree Programs in English of the Federation of North Texas Area Universities, 1976), p. 41.

guage. But we would have to go further. We would have to refer to respect for authority, propriety of actions (recall the picture of one student sitting in President Grayson Kirk's chair smoking one of the president's own cigars), appropriateness of dress—in fact, we would have to include an entire value system of one segment of society at that time as opposed to that of another. The words "Up against the wall, Mother!" symbolized the new value system that had broken the norms of the old.

Whatever is a norm in a particular society cannot be represented graphically by a single dot. It has to be a series of dots; that is, it has to be thought of as a range—a range representing degrees of tolerance among individuals, a range allowing for differences of temperament among people, a range recognizing economic, educational, and cultural variations—yet, significantly, a range of sufficient commonness to represent what we refer to as the "prevailing tone," "the temper of the times," or "acceptable standards." As elusive as normative standards appear to be, they are there. They are the basis for our emotional responses to language and actions. Some things upset us by being excessive. Others bore us by being deficient. Either extreme exceeds our range of tolerance. Either extreme upsets our equilibrium. Either extreme "goes too far," as we commonly say. Our intuitive sense of the normative has been violated.

Writers concerned about being read and accepted also have to concern themselves about normative reactions; that is, these writers have to operate within a generalized range of tolerance. Experimental writers speak of the mass audience as an enemy of innovation and change. Essentially, that is true. Readers prefer to be comfortable, to be pleased. Writers who want to be popular have to cater to popular norms. Writers who are innovative in style necessarily appeal to a small group of readers until such time as their newness no longer exceeds the limits of normative standards. The history of prevailing taste in writing may be described as a record of the shifting range of normative values. The teaching of writing in the schools has always been highly normative. At any particular time, however, writers who want to create a sensation, stir up feelings, or vent their anger can do so easily enough by adopting an extreme stance or by using language that seems prevailingly immoderate. Essentially, breaking the norm is an anti-rhetorical stance. It puts a barrier between reader and writer.

What is the mark of controversy? What is the measure of excess or deficiency? Essentially anything that exceeds our threshold of tolerance. Some people might want to talk of these matters in terms of a "sense of appropriateness," although appropriateness or suitability is not necessarily a matter of intuition. A number of obvious things can be prescribed: avoid obscenities at church gatherings, avoid pious phrases at pot parties, avoid frivolities on solemn occasions, avoid solemnities on light-hearted occasions. These are social commonplaces that hardly demand intuitive sensibility. Yet there are other decisions about language of greater subtlety that taboos do not cover. What do we mean when we say someone overwrites? Or is too cute with language? Or pompous? We recognize these traits in others. Can we sense them in ourselves and in our own writing? How do we know when we or others are being patronizing or pretentious? Or jargonish? Or overly techincal? These are all total effects that result not from the use of single words but from the combinations of words and structures, producing a tone that is in terms of the audience either "in tune" or "out of tune." Tone should be a subject for discussion in the classroom. We have to learn from others—not from the teacher alone—what is "out of tune," where a writer has slipped beyond the range of tolerance, where audience receptivity ends, when eccentricity becomes absurd, when flamboyance produces delight or disgust, how constant cautiousness becomes dullness, when disagreement becomes hostility—whether these, in fact, are effects the writer intends. Talking about the limits of the range is a way of recognizing that a normative sense operates in the judgments we make. It is a way of informing intuition.

The second intuitive sense I would like to identify—the sense of simplicity—may very well be a subcategory of the first, but the overlap only means that one intuitive response is not separate and discrete from another, nor are particular senses limited to just one mode such as writing or music or dance. What we recognize as simple about a picture may not be basically different in principle from what is simple about writing or a melody or the facade of a building.

In writing, a certain kind of simplicity can be achieved by prescriptions that we are all familiar with: avoid big words, avoid foreign phrases, avoid coinages, avoid constructions with *there is* and *there are*, avoid long sentences—the list might be lengthened considerably. Like many prescriptions, these are often counter-intuitive. Further, too great an emphasis on taboos causes some students to regress. If we create the idea that simplicity means merely syntactic plainness, they will substitute primer sentences for structures more characteristic of mature writers. Clearly, simplicity does not mean childishness.

In *Simple & Direct*, Jacques Barzun writes as follows:

> Before discussing a number of tones encountered in the prose of today, I want to lay it down as an axiom that the best tone is the tone called plain, unaffected, unadorned. It does not talk down or jazz up; it assumes the equality of all readers likely to approach the given subject; it informs or argues without apologizing for its task; it does not try to dazzle or cajole the indifferent; it takes no posture of coziness or sophistication. It is the most difficult of all tones, and also the most adaptable.[9]

Clearly, Barzun is talking about simplicity as a norm, something like the knob on a stereo set that indicates balance—and then all degrees of volume and tone are tuned according to one's tastes. In these terms, our intuitive sense of simplicity is a sense that helps to keep us on balance. But how?

I would like to define simplicity as the most economical way to get the highest return. Economy in writing depends upon sharp perception, unambiguous words, and unforced syntax. Ultimately, the test is not long or short sentences, but sentences that are clear and precise; not big words or little words, but words that are familiar and understandable. The enemy of simplicity is the thesaurus.

---

[9](New York: Harper & Row, 1975), p. 91.

The ultimate in simplicity is contained in one verse of the New Testament of the Bible, simply "Jesus wept." It is the most economical expression one might conceive, yet one of the richest in its implications. The spare phrasing yields a high return. It expresses a depth of meaning and emotion. True, the implications grow out of the total context; knowing the whole story is part of the dramatic impact of the sentence. Yet it is important to note how this particular sentence, not a different one, creates its effect. We would only detract from the economy and the simplicity if we added even one word: "Jesus wept profusely" or "Jesus wept, heartbroken." Nothing is added by these extra words. More is not necessary because the verb alone expresses the essence of the experience. This is simplicity.

Plainness, however, should not be consistently identified with simplicity. Far more complex sentences may be both simple and readable. On the topic of readability, Chapters 4 and 5 of *The Philosophy of Composition* by E. D. Hirsch, Jr., are particularly instructive. If readability is defined as reading ease, it should follow that the easiest is best. We also have to acknowledge that primer sentences are easiest. But they are also boring. Without actually saying so in his discussion, Hirsch suggests that readability indexes—those measurements of reading ease—lead to a logical absurdity because they do not take into account meaning and intention. He proposes a new term that does: relative readability. He says, "Assuming that two texts convey the same meaning, the more readable text will take less time and effort to understand."[10] Relative readability is "the most efficient communication of *any* semantic intention."[11] He concedes that no two texts can convey the same meaning exactly, but "the question we mainly want to ask is whether a piece of writing conveys its meaning without hindrance from the author's carelessness, ineptitude, or lack of craft." Hirsch's concept

---

[10] E. D. Hirsch, Jr., *The Philosophy of Composition* (Chicago: University of Chicago Press, 1977), p. 85.

[11] Hirsch, p. 75.

of relative readability and my own definition of simplicity correspond to one another. We are both speaking of the easiest manner (the most readable way) consistent with the author's intentions, although when Hirsch cites Faulkner as an author "not very readable on an absolute scale," but high ranking in relative readability,[12] I would be hard pressed to characterize Faulkner's prose as simple. However laudable Faulkner's intentions may be, the obstacles to readability in the prose remain. Whatever his virtues, Faulkner lacks a sense of simplicity.

It might be appropriately pointed out here that the short sentence is not a necessary condition of simplicity. Further, the tightest version of a sentence (shades of "Omit needless words") is not necessarily the most readable. Meanings are often more readily accessible if there are filler words. Consider the ambiguities of telegrams and headlines. They are occasionally too abbreviated to be clear. Brevity and readability are not one and the same.

Simplicity, plainness, readability, brevity, and clarity are terms that cannot be used interchangeably. Barzun is undoubtedly right when he says the simple style is the most difficult to achieve, particularly if we bring into play a third sense: our sense of rhythm. It is one of the most important of our intuitive senses in producing readable prose and the sense least susceptible to either prescription or proscription. In fact, most books on writing say little or nothing about prose rhythm except to include a few remarks about alliteration, balanced structures, and placement of words for purposes of emphasis. Left undiscussed are terms like timing or pace or movement or proportion. Yet these are essential to prose rhythm, undoubtedly left unmentioned because they can hardly be talked about except in terms of an intuitive sense of rhythm.

Scattered attempts to treat prose rhythm as a teachable subject inevitably get around to scanning, as if prose were written in meter like verse. Scanning of prose in terms of traditional

---

[12] Hirsch, p. 75.

feet is consistently unsatisfactory because, while it may account for the memorableness or quotability of a particular phrase, it fails to account for the way writers write readable prose. Such writers seem to be listening to an inner drum. Rhythm is basic to all movement, whether our own or nature's—the wind swaying the trees or water lapping the shore. If we reflect upon various movements, we will become more consciously aware of the extent to which we are influenced by balance—one thing, then another; one thing against another in equal proportion.

The most extensive study of prose rhythm I know is a doctoral dissertation by Regina Hoover based on a computer analysis of approximately 90,000 words of nonfiction prose. Hoover proposes a principle of proportional distribution in prose rhythm. Saying that English is basically an iambic language cannot be supported by her data. She suggests that we respond more spontaneously to a one-to-two distribution (one stress to two unstressed syllables) than to a one-to-one distribution (one stress to one unstressed). She resorts to metaphor to clarify: "Possibly one can better explain the sense of English rhythm by using the metaphor of a scale; the stressed syllable on one side must be balanced by more than one nonstressed syllable on the other. But because the stresses given to syllables are variable in our language, we can adjust to small variations; the ratio does not have to be exactly one-to-two."[13] What we seek in prose rhythm is a kind of rhythmic completion in the same way that we want chords to be resolved harmonically. In my own writing experience, I have never scanned sentences to get them "right," but I have read them aloud, and I have read them silently with an awareness of an inner rhythmic sense that either approves or disapproves.

Once we accept an intuitive basis for the rhythm of sentences, it follows that a comparable principle of proportional distribution operates in larger units as well. Paragraphing is a

---

[13]"Prose Rhythm: A Theory of Proportional Distribution," *College Composition and Communication,* 24 (1973), 374.

way of varying the pace and rhythm of an entire composition. An essay without rhythmic variation in its larger units grows tedious in the same way that sentences unvaried in their rhythmic patterns grow monotonous. Movement is more than an ordering of parts in a particular direction. That is a physical description of the way sentences and paragraphs look on the page. From within, movement is a rhythmic pattern, indivisible and continuous. Intuition perceives it as a whole, not as pieces patched together.

But can we also instruct this intuitive sense? Perhaps the most direct thing we can do is to encourage oral reading in the schools, not just of essays that students write, but of published essays by other writers. At the present, one of the most embarrassing things a college instructor can do in class is to ask a student to read a passage of prose aloud. In practically four cases out of five, the result is a hesitant, stumbling performance. Since I am not interested in humiliating students in this way, the alternative is simply not to ask anyone to read. Yet the connection between that kind of oral performance and an intuitive perception of rhythm ought to be obvious: there cannot be much feeling for the movement of language if someone has to stumble word by word through a passage.

Yet it must be conceded that many people who cannot read aloud satisfactorily do have an intuitive sense of rhythm. The intuitive senses are not the resources of writers only. Swimmers, violinists, carpenters, and dancers are all caught up in rhythmic movements that are basic to their success. More and more we need to make individuals aware that one part of their lives has connection with another part. Running and writing are not wholly separated. A track man needs to be convinced that he might apply the concept of pacing in long-distance running to a prose composition. A singer who knows the stunning effect of a rest in music ought to appreciate the importance of juncture in writing. We categorize our activities to such an extent that we fail to see meaningful correspondences. Often students need only to be reminded of these analogues to make full use of their intuitive resources.

The kind of rhythmic wholeness I have been speaking of is also complemented by a fourth intuitive sense: our sense of order. It reveals itself in a number of different ways: first, in beginning (where is the appropriate starting point?), then, in sequence (what things naturally and logically follow one another?), in connection (what bridges are necessary to tie things together?), in dimension and proportion (how should the space be distributed among the parts?), and finally in closing (how do we recognize when we have come to the end of something?). This kind of listing of things we do intuitively indicates how complex the matter of ordering and shaping is. If we had to think of each of these steps in turn, we would flounder in the act of writing. But we don't. We write as if ordering were one function, just as we walk without thinking about every movement. Even though we as teachers at times focus on parts of this total ordering—on transitions, for instance—writers move through the whole process guided by their intuitive sense of order. Those who lack that grasp stumble along the way. They labor the beginning; they omit transitions because they lack a sense of continuity; they fail to recognize the imbalance of parts because they lack a sense of proportion; they fail to recognize that they have not finished because they lack a sense of closure, a sense that tells us that the parts have or have not been molded together into a satisfying unit.

As human beings, we are not born with an innate sense of shape and structure. We don't begin with an inborn abstraction of form and order. As infants, we begin with tactile exploration and at more mature stages gradually begin to form concepts of mass and contour and depth and pattern. These become the intuitive basis of our sense of order. In an essay written in 1959, Hans Freudenthal refers to the average man "whose intuitive space has been molded by our straight streets flanked by parallel walls, and by the experience of all those products of technology that suggest to him the validity of the Euclidean axioms."[14] In

---

[14]Quoted by Mario Bunge, *Intuition and Science* (Englewood Cliffs, N.J.: Prentice-Hall, 1962), p. 64.

Western culture, our concept of order is closely tied to qualities of linearity and symmetricality. In terms of writing, what most of us recognize as logical is a one-directional sequence of thoughts with parts connected link by link to form continuous, successive discourse. If any of the links are missing, we dismiss the chain of reasoning as weak. A *non sequitur* is an illogical intrusion. Quite literally, "it does not follow" in terms of linear development.

Once we have acquired a structural model, we are able to function intuitively. In recent years I have asked several hundred students to describe what they do when they write, not what they think they should do or what they tell others to do, but what they actually do. Almost to a person, they talk about the difficulties of getting started. In fact, most of the narratives tell about ways to procrastinate. Once started, however, they proceed with greater ease, like a car moving through the gears to "drive." A sense of progression takes over. One thing suggests another by association. One thing leads to another by logical relationship. In an article entitled "Sentences in Action," Richard Larson lists some of these functions and relationships.[15] He calls them the "roles" that sentences play. But they do happen "in action." In the act of composing, the development sentence by sentence does not usually occur as a series of conscious decisions. They are intuitive ones.

Finally, like driving a car, almost no one has too much trouble knowing when to stop. As writers, we ordinarily know when we have arrived where we intended to go. What we anticipated has been fulfilled. Our sense of closure is intuitive. Acting intuitively in such matters requires a faithfulness to our own insights. We need to emphasize that fact over and over to give individuals the kind of certainty they need to become confident writers.

The four intuitive senses I have separated here for purposes of discussion—a sense of the normative, a sense of sim-

---

[15]*College Composition and Communication*, 18 (1967), 16-22.

plicity, a sense of rhythm, and a sense of order—may be complements of one another. In fact, I am certain they are. Further, they combine to form the basis of our aesthetic faculty. They help to develop our sensitivity to qualities that please us. They define the values that give us a sense of well-being. In the preface to *Sight and Insight*, Richard Guggenheimer refers to the neglect of what he calls "aesthetic literacy."[16] Surely, a fuller awareness of our intuitive senses can act as a corrective to that form of neglect.

Recognizing the role of intuition in writing should not be thought of as an easy solution to the teaching problem. The hard fact remains that both teachers and students are distrustful of references to intuition. Teachers hesitate to talk about the undemonstrable. The result is that many things students are asked to do or told not to do are counter-intuitive. Students, not adequately recognizing that learning to write is mainly learning to trust themselves, want someone to tell them what to do. Surely any composition course ought to begin with a description or discussion of the kind of activity we are concerned with when we write. Learning to write is the long process of what Ray Bradbury calls "feeding a Muse."[17] Writing is drawing upon the intuitive resources we store. As we store, so shall we write.

---

[16]*Sight and Insight: A Prediction of New Perceptions in Art* (New York: Harper, 1945), p. viii.

[17]"How to Keep and Feed a Muse," *The Writer*, 74 (1961), 7-12.

5

Who Is a Good
Composition Teacher?

During the 1960s, Don Eulert undertook a three-year project at Wisconsin State University at Platteville to determine why certain students improved in their writing ability, while others with essentially the same background, intelligence, and training did not. His conclusion is stated briefly: "The Wisconsin study showed that nearly 70 percent of student performance could be predicted by items measuring, for the most part, a student's attitudes and values. Performance cannot be so accurately predicted by items usually considered significant, such as the number of themes written, grading techniques, type and amount of grammar, or even percentile rank and intelligence."[1] Learning, he goes on to say, takes place primarily when the student's ego, attitudes, and motivation are engaged. Other factors are negligible.

Some scholars dismiss Eulert's findings because of an inad-

---

[1] "The Relationship of Personality Factors to Learning in College Composition," *College Composition and Communication*, 18 (1967), 62.

equate research design, and some teachers deplore the behavioral implications—"the business of manipulating students," as Eulert phrases it. Nevertheless, the Eulert study is highly instructive, and I have come to accept his general conclusions, first, because I think they are intuitively sound and, second, because I have confirmed them by my own observations and experience. These, then, are my own thoughts about teaching in the composition classroom.

I am convinced that the single most important factor that affects improvement in the composition class is the teacher-student relationship. All teachers in a program may use the same text, all may provide essentially the same information and instruction, all may require the same amount of writing; yet some will get results and some will not. In short, the personality and attitudes of the teacher will be a stronger influence than any of the materials.

Having said that, it might follow that we could define the ideal composition teacher. But that does not follow, because successful teachers vary in personality and temperament from quiet, introspective types to highly vocal, flamboyant types. And their own self-confidence may depend entirely upon their know-how, derived either from formal training or experience. One of the sober realities of English teaching is that every teacher is expected at one time or another to be a composition teacher. The question is not to determine who is ideal and who is not, but to identify the qualities that good teachers seem to share, attitudes that make a difference to students, and attributes that give the relationship between teacher and student a working chance.

I began the Introduction to this book with the sentence: "I take the teaching of writing seriously." I wanted to say that first because I think it is of first importance in any writing course. Teachers have to take the course seriously, and students have to also. What we often find, however, is a combination of indifference—teachers doing with their left hand what is required of them, students doing perfunctorily what may also be required of them but, if it is not, doing something that seems not to have the same practical value as computer programming or laboratory dissection. Teachers have to help students change their attitude toward their performance before they can actually change their performance. This is true of all students, but particularly of those who know before they start that they will be losers again. Most remedial programs simply do not work because the students never emerge from the morass of their own feelings of failure.

A good teacher knows the difference between expectation and intimidation. Expectation operates by encouragement. It encourages stretching, a realization of the student's potential. Intimidation works by fear. It fosters stagnation by forcing students simply to do what has been prescribed. The teacher's commitment to the job is communicative, sometimes by intensity, sometimes by enthusiasm, sometimes by the energy that is being expended. A lack of commitment also becomes obvious, even though the teacher may not be openly negligent. Needless to say, the indifference of a teacher encourages dull, indifferent writing.

Closely related to the teacher's attitude toward the course—the job of teaching writing—is the teacher's assumptions about the students in a composition class. Aren't most of them there because they have to be? Aren't they more interested in other courses like chemistry or sociology? In fact, aren't they more interested in their friends than in studies? In TV? In cars? In sports? Assume these things, and they will be self-fulfilling. A good teacher begins with belief—belief that writing can be taught and that it is worth teaching. Begin with apologies, and the tone will be set. I know one instructor who began the quarter by saying, "I know you don't want to be here, and I don't either, but we'll have to make the best of it." Then he wondered why "the best" wasn't better than it was.

A good teacher is one who cares and one for whom students care. These are not meant to be Valentine sentiments. They translate into everyday terms. A teacher who is not concerned enough to give students topics that they can write about cannot expect them to care enough to make something of nothing. A teacher who is not concerned enough to react to student writing cannot expect students to want to try harder next time. Encouragement and positive reinforcement are best, but outrage will sometimes work. Now some thirty years later I still remember a marginal notation on one of my graduate papers. One of my contorted sentences prompted the professor to write "Ugh!" I can't praise that as the most tactful comment he could have made; it didn't please me, but I haven't forgotten it. What the comment signified was that he cared enough to indicate a kind of revulsion, exaggerated though it may have been. Unfortunately, in his case, most of his reactions were negative, but I learned in later years that he was a person who cared immensely about writing. I learned too that I didn't want that kind of reaction to my own writing, and I learned that I had to care if I wanted to avoid monstrosities.

Caring need not mean chumminess, although the teacher-student relationship presents all kinds of temptations. Time will not eliminate the chances of students getting crushes on teachers or teachers succumbing to youthful beauty, but these are not major problems. What is major is sensing the distance a student requires. Most students will signal their preference for an appropriate distance. A good teacher has a sensing device to know how much distance to keep, not categorically deciding remoteness is safe. Aloofness is safe, to be sure, but it may also be damaging to the relationship. Any *a priori* decision to be intimate or reserved is simply ignoring the fact that putting twenty-five people in a composition classroom doesn't make them all alike. A good teacher recognizes diversity in students and works with the grain that they show, not against it, to turn their natural tendencies to advantage.

No teacher can escape entirely the image of the authority figure, no matter how close that teacher chooses to be to students. Teachers give grades. They are in charge. Traditionally, the teacher is the one who knows and the students are those who do not, although a composition class actually allows that fundamental distinction to be broken if teacher and student think of themselves as actively working together as co-writers. I have often heard young actors acknowledge their indebtedness to older, more experienced actors with whom they have had the "privilege of working" (as they usually say). A teacher-student relationship ought to be something comparable. It ought to be a privilege to work together—on both sides. Or it ought to be more like student and technician working together in the laboratory than an adversary relationship that the traditional class situation too often fosters.

Above all, it is important that negative feelings be averted in a teacher-student relation. If circumstances or personalities do not permit positive feelings, then they should at least be neutral. Teachers who can't be loved can at least earn respect. Contempt negates a relationship completely. Through the years, as I have received complaints from students about particular teachers, I have almost inevitably learned after a few probing questions that what the students like to call a "personlity conflict" isn't a clash of personalities at all; it is a lack of respect for one another. The student has decided that the teacher is too youthful, too inexperienced, too haughty, or too demanding. The teacher has decided the student is hopelessly unprepared, unteachable, or lazy. They are incapable of working together, not particularly because they clash temperamentally, but because neither fits the preconceived image of the other.

As much as a student's ego is a crucial ingredient in writing, so also is a teacher's ego for success in teaching. Every teacher needs an ego charged enough to be felt. I do not refer to forceful personalities, histrionic types, or eccentrics. They often intimidate students and discourage them from open expression. Students are afraid to put their own egos on the battleline with a supercharged person. Frequently, very gentle, introspective people—not to be confused with weak or ineffectual people— make remarkably good composition teachers, chiefly because they seem unthreatening. But showy or quiet, all teachers have to project; that is, they have to be sending out messages of confidence—confidence in themselves and confidence in students. They cannot be immersed in themselves, talking as it were to themselves. Teaching is a communicative act. Where no communication occurs, no learning occurs.

In one of his well-known essays, Wayne Booth defines the true rhetorical stance as "a stance which depends on discovering and maintaining in any writing situation a proper balance among three elements that are at work in a communicative effort: the available arguments about the subject itself, the interests and peculiarities of the audience, and the voice, the implied character of the speaker."[2] Unbalancing the stance in favor of any one component becomes a corruption. Booth speaks of three: the advertiser's stance, preferring effect to substance; the pedant's stance, expounding the subject and forgetting the audience; and the entertainer's stance, projecting more personality than substance.

Booth's discussion provides a model for what we might call the true "teaching stance," one that ideally maintains a proper balance among the role of the teacher, the available knowledge to be learned about the subject, and the needs and interests of the students. The corruptions are the same. Among teachers, we all know the advertisers, the pedants, and the entertainers. Good writing teachers make their presence felt, but do not dominate. They maintain that there is a body of knowledge to be learned, but acknowledge that just knowing facts will not produce better writers. They recognize that students learn best by participating and discovering on their own; that development depends on reinforcement. All three are necessary in proper balance.

One of the pleasant assurances about writing a chapter of this kind is that I can be confident there are people who do not fit the pattern of these remarks, yet prove to be amazingly effective teachers. But I have learned to be skeptical of self-announced effectiveness. When anybody tells me that he or she has had a remarkably successful quarter, my first response is to

---

[2]"The Rhetorical Stance," *College Composition and Communication*, 14 (1963), 141.

ask, "What did you do?" The crucial question in teaching composition is not "What works?" Students are adept at jumping
through hoops if the teacher requires them to do so. Many
approaches work. That's what some people call "success"—getting students to do what is asked of them. The crucial question
is not "What works?" but "What helps?" Does it help to reinforce taboos, for instance? I once had a teacher who permitted
no one to use the word *feel* to refer to cognition. If anyone
wrote "I feel that the moral climate in the nation is improving,"
feel would be crossed out and *think* substituted. What this
teacher's dogmatism did, of course, was to limit the use of the
word *feel* to the expression of sensation or emotion, denying a
perfectly legitimate use of the word as a synonym for *believe*,
not a purely rational act, but one combining thinking and feeling. I remember another instructor who passed out a ditto of
some thirty to fifty words and phrases that could not be used in
themes. Many of them were common words and phrases like
"field," "factor," "in fact," "in my opinion," "there is," "seemingly"—admittedly words and phrases often overused or used in
jargonish ways, but similarly often indispensable. This instructor's list had no qualifications or allowances, just "Don't use
them." Taboos are meant to create guilt. Some people have
accumulated so many guilt feelings through years of school that
they are afraid to put words on paper. Every word is a damnable
trap.

Every answer to "What helps?" therefore needs to be
tested by one other question: "What harms?" The answers are
many: Whatever intervenes between teacher and student.
Whatever creates fear. Whatever inhibits openness. Whatever
discourages positive motivation. Whatever demands too little or
too much. Whatever threatens the writer's ego. Impossible conditions to meet? Not really. A little humanity and sensitivity on
the part of a teacher will go far to assure students that they have
as much freedom of expression in the classroom as they do
outside the classroom.

Part III

THE PRACTICE

Introduction to Part II

The chapters in Part II place a strong emphasis on the practice of teaching composition. What do you do besides ask students to write and then read their writing? Of course, writing itself is the most important thing they do, and Chapter 6 suggests that a class might be converted entirely into a writing workshop, where students do little more than write, just as pianists play music in their practice rooms or as chemists test, measure, and observe in their laboratories. But, as we well know, workshops and laboratories provide more than opportunities for practice. They ordinarily include a series of related and meaningful exercises. The composition classroom can become the same kind of learning session.

I would hasten immediately to differentiate between two kinds of exercises: first, those that attempt to reinforce learning by repetition (we are most familiar with these as workbook exercises) and, second, those that are based upon a principle of discovery (students are asked to pursue a particular project as a way of getting them to come to some realization on their own.)

The second especially are pedagogical means of helping stu
dents develop their intuitive resources.

Since exercises of the first variety are plentiful in most text
books, the following chapters will concentrate on projects of the
second variety. The two key words are discovery and awareness.
Each project should aim at creating a new awareness by some
discovery. We need to remind ourselves that what is old to us
may be a revelation to someone else. Or a project may cause us
to see something familiar in a fresh way. If projects have no
discernible purpose, students will then pursue them only as busy
work. I happen to think that lecturing has no place in the composition classroom. A lecture on various concepts of style might
be of interest to a few students, but it will not help many of
them develop a more mature prose style. They are more likely
to learn something about style by writing first and then talking
about possible variations. Clearly, teachers need to comment
and explain, but informal presentations lasting 10 or 20 minutes
are quite different from 50-minute lectures, prepared with notes
or written to be read.

Teaching by the project/discovery method is not easy.
First, it requires some theoretical understanding on the part of
the instructor about the things students need. What they need
is not always what the instructor plans to give them. Dorothy
Guinn has published an article entitled "Freshman Composition: The Right Texts but the Wrong Students Walk in the
Door."[1] That is too often the dilemma. The instructor has to
know how to adapt material to the students who walk in the
door. That may mean doing something different in a 10:30 class
from what went on at 9:30.

Second, the project/discovery method requires a good bit
of dittoing. I must confess that I could not teach composition
without a ditto machine, chiefly because I think students should
be able to see each other's writing so that they can reflect on it.
Dittoing, as we know, takes time, and it has to be done in ad-

---

[1] *College Composition and Communication*, 27(1976), 344-349.

vance. As far as I'm concerned, however, it is worth the effort. A ditto also provides the first condition for a good discussion: it allows me to keep quiet to give students a chance to talk.

As soon as students recognize by the extent of preparation going on that an instructor cares, they will respond in kind. Composition classes don't have to be Mickey Mouse affairs. They can offer students challenging assignments that are intellectually stimulating and practically valuable.

6

Planning a Course

For best results, instruction in writing has to begin as early as possible in elementary school and continue. Further, the type of writing asked for should correspond to the primary interests of most children at a particular age. Thus, most beginners delight in narration and description, telling what they have done or whom they have seen. By the time young people have reached high school age, they should be writing something besides their autobiographies for the fourth or fifth time. At that level, they should know how to use narration for expository purposes; that is, to be able to narrate an anecdote as an example or use illustration for support of a general thesis. Fortunately, we never outgrow our interest in narrative, but we can learn to put it to new purposes.

If in junior high school or middle school, students write their first "research paper," a paper based on library sources, they should learn précis writing at that point—and not later. They should know how to summarize, how to paraphrase, and how to take notes. At the present time, many college students get their first formal instruction in research paper writing during their second quarter or semester of freshman composition. Plagiarism is an epidemic in some colleges, not always because of deliberate dishonesty, but simply because of ignorance and complete lack of confidence. Students have not been taught to read, to absorb, and to restate in their own words the ideas and opinions of other writers.

Experienced teachers at various grade levels should be the best judges of what to emphasize. When young teenagers, for instance, delight in puns and rhymes, they should be given a free hand to play with language. The problem of many dull writers at a later stage is that they think of language only as a tool, and accordingly use it like a mallet to pound away. They have never experienced the fun of using language in novel ways. At a stage when young children are most inquisitive, they should be made aware that their questions—to others and to themselves—are the source of their ideas. Or, perhaps at another stage, that observation sharpens detail. Or, still further along, that analogies increase our understanding.

For a number of years in a student survey of our Freshman English courses at the University of Washington we have had a question that reads: "Do you think your Freshman English course was unduly repetitious of your high school English course?" The replies are overwhelmingly negative, but those who answer "Yes" are invited to say why. A large percentage of these answers say that the course was just more reading and writing. That pleases me. If composition courses are repetitious in any way, they ought to be repetitious by asking for "more reading and writing." As they repeat, they need not duplicate the same experience. A writing curriculum ought to be thought of as an inverted cone—an ever-increasing spiral, another time around, but always changing planes and widening the writer's scope.

But what about the routine? Do the courses through the years have a sameness? Yes, if at each succeeding level they include the same tired topics that students have written on many times before. Otherwise, writing can be a new experience each time—to this extent. If writing is a mode of behavior, as I have predicated, it then changes as the individual develops. Writing ability is more likely to grow by leaps than by steps. My own experience causes me to think of writing progress in terms of plateaus—individual ones, not collective ones. A student reaches a plateau at a particular age or grade level and may very well stay there until he or she has lived longer, read more, experienced more, and thought more about living. It is clear that some people get stuck at a particular level, not because they lack instruction, but because they fail to respond. Teaching composition—perhaps like all teaching—is a two-way affair. Teachers have responsibilities. So do students. Students consistently know what the teachers' responsibilities are. They don't always think about what theirs are.

In well-coordinated English programs at the secondary level, curriculum guides sometimes provide a special focus for a particular grade level, perhaps grammar, mechanics, sentence-combining, paragraphing, or some other emphasis. My own observation is that a great deal of autonomy prevails among teachers. Not much articulation (that symbolic term for an orderly education) goes on. We also have to face the fact that the emphasis at a particular grade level is often determined by the available textbooks on the shelves. In any case, the issue of the total English curriculum is beyond the scope of this book. I would like to say a few things, however, about the kind of unit or course that is given over exclusively to writing for a period of ten to fourteen weeks. Where does one start? What does one do?

Undoubtedly, the previous discussion has made clear that when we write we are totally involved with the process from the moment we begin. We cannot be concerned with words alone. Everything impinges at once: thoughts, emotions, structures, modes, and the transcription itself. In fairly technical discussions, the process is characterized as holistic. And it might seem to follow that what is holistic ought to be taught in a holistic way, that is, as an entity. I am not aware how that is possible. As fully as I acknowledge that we do not explain everything about writing when we talk about it in piecemeal fashion, it is the only way of talking specifically about what is right and what is faulty. We may want our students to be better writers, but if we can't get at the cause of a problem in particular terms, then we are not likely to help. In outlining a unit or course, I am therefore focusing on parts of the process, trusting that attention to each part will contribute something to the total blend. It works in cooking. It can work in teaching, too.

Customarily, writing courses progress in either of two general ways: from the whole to the parts or from the parts to the whole. The first approach assumes that the students can already write a composition, however good or bad. They are asked to do that, and the course then begins to focus in turn on organization, paragraphing, sentence structure, word choice, and details of mechanics. The second approach is basically a building-block approach from words to sentences to paragraphs to the total essay, as if the process of writing and the actual transcription on paper were one and the same, for we do proceed in this way when we put words down on paper. The first approach actually parallels the writing process. It recognizes motive and situation as the starting point. It permits individuals to write intuitively in terms of their own purposes and then focus with a degree of objectivity upon the way the parts work together.

It is not really profitable to argue the merits of one approach or the other, because teachers who have adopted one of them are usually convinced of its value and are not likely to change. They may actually use a blend of the two, what might be a consideration of parts and wholes simultaneously or at least of the relation of parts to the whole. The organizational scheme of a writing course is arbitrary. Whether it is one way or another is not as important as that there be *some* way. In my own training program, I require all assistants first to try a scheme that I outline and describe to them. I then give them the option in subsequent quarters of making adjustments that they want to make. We then talk about why they changed what they did. Most of the reasons fall into the general category of expediency: their students needed this or that earlier in the quarter. Meeting urgent needs is all right, of course, as long as it doesn't signify that we are always reviewing—going backward instead of forward.

Here is one tried and workable plan that lends itself to multiple variations. It begins with the writer as a person, focuses on the writer in action, and finishes with the written product, separated from the writer and ready for reading. These do not have to be considered equal time units. The first main topic may well be done in two or three days, whereas the third may take four weeks. The questions are intended to suggest a range of subtopics for consideration and discussion. They include some subjects we have already covered in Part I of this book. Others will be treated in subsequent chapters.

    I. The Persona: the writer
        A. Attitudes toward writing and the role of the teacher: the writer's sense of purpose
            What is the nature of writing?
            How is writing learned?
            What do students expect from the course?
            What do they think the teacher can do?
            What can the teacher do?
            What is the relation of motive to progress?
        B. Attitudes toward language and its function: varieties of usage
            Is language only a tool?
            What are the intrinsic and extrinsic values of language?
            What is usage as opposed to grammar?
            In what instances does "correctness" apply?
            What does "standard English" signify?
            What other varieties of English are there?
        C. Differences between thinking, talking, and writing: the element of control
            What are various words we use for forms of thinking?
            What differences do these words imply?
            What happens when people talk?
            What happens when people write?
            What are the special demands of writing?
            Do the demands vary with different kinds of writing?

　　D. Finding a voice: relation of feeling, voice, and tone
　　　　How do we indicate feeling and tone in speaking?
　　　　How does tone emerge in writing?
　　　　What is a persona? How do we identify it?
　　　　Is the "one true self" a fact or illusion?
　　　　What is the relation of voice to an identifiable style?
　　　　What do we mean by the Plain Style?
II. Process
　　A. Pre-writing
　　　　1. Inventiveness: ways of generating ideas
　　　　　　What is the merit of "forced thinking" or "automatic writing"?
　　　　　　What is the advantage of paradigms, matrixes, or models as an aid to thinking?
　　　　　　What other techniques promote inventiveness?
　　　　2. Judging ideas: selecting and focusing
　　　　　　Is an idea different from a thought?
　　　　　　What is a good idea for purposes of writing?
　　　　　　How do ideas originate?
　　　　　　What is a cliché-thought as opposed to a cliché-expression?
　　　　　　What are the criteria for selecting and focusing?
　　　　　　What does unity mean in terms of writing?
　　　　3. Structuring ideas: a plan
　　　　　　What set forms are available?
　　　　　　What are the advantages and disadvantages of set forms?
　　　　　　What functions does formal outlining have?
　　　　　　What does "writing as discovery" mean?
　　　　　　What do "linear" and "nonlinear" mean as applied to various art forms?
　　　　　　What do they mean as applied to writing?
　　B. Intuition as a factor in writing
　　　　How does intuition function?
　　　　How do we develop intuitive resources?
　　　　In what way does intuition relate to a writer's individual development?
　　　　Is intuition the "mystery" of writing?
　　C. Considerations of audience: accommodation and appropriateness
　　　　Who represents an audience?

How does a writer write for an audience if the audience is unknown?

How does a writer create an audience?

What can a writer do to appeal to readers?

Do we write the same on all occasions?

III. Product: rhetoric and style in terms of strategy
    A. Patterns of thought: paragraphing

Does paragraphing vary with different forms of writing (journalism, fiction, essay)?

What do paragraphs do? What purposes do they serve?

In what way is paragraphing like punctuation?

Do paragraphs follow a set form? Are there patterns?

In what ways can paragraphs be developed?

    B. Sentence strategy

What are the basic sentence patterns?

In what ways can they be varied?

What are the common rhetorical types?

How does context affect sentence construction?

    C. Word strategy

What do word labels (slang, jargon, technical, archaic) signify?

How do words change categories?

What is the relation of sound to word arrangement?

How can emphasis be gained by word arrangement?

What determines appropriateness of word choice?

What is a writer's idiolect?

    D. Punctuation strategy

What are the basic uses of the individual marks?

Are some marks related to one another? Are they at times interchangeable?

In what sense is the use of punctuation a stylistic element?

I would again point to a problem many people find difficult to cope with: even though students are concerned with all of these topics from the first day that they write, the teacher cannot talk about everything at once, either in class or even individually to students through comments. The focus has to shift. A shifting focus gives students a chance to concentrate on one thing at a time.

These same topics can be rearranged into other organizational plans. In skeletal form, here are several others. The subtopics would remain essentially the same.

One that uses the familiar communication triangle:

I. The Writer: Pre-writing
II. The Composition: Strategy and Style
III. The Audience: Appropriateness

One that uses Kenneth Burke's pentad:

I. Agent: The Writer
II. Purpose of Writing
III. Scene: Audience
IV. Act: The Process of Writing
  A. Pre-writing
  B. Structuring
  C. Reasoning
V. Agency or means:
  A. Paragraph strategy
  B. Sentence strategy
  C. Word strategy
  D. Mechanics

One that focuses on the writer:

I. The Writer's Voice and Feeling
II. The Writer's Ideas
III. The Writer's Plan
IV. The Writer's Words
V. The Writer's Strategies
VI. The Writer's Style

These plans assume that the teacher conducts—or is required to conduct—formal classroom sessions. The course as a whole therefore has a sense of direction and purpose. A small class conducted on a tutorial basis can clearly be more efficient because a teacher needs to emphasize only what an individual needs. Classroom instruction tends to be scattershot. A third alternative is to conduct a writing class as a workshop, a place where students go to write, just as members of a chorus go to class to sing. Students can confer with an "editor" about their writing when they wish. The "editor" can be the teacher or another student. In such a setting, students have a chance to think of their writing in professional terms, not in schoolroom terms. The workshop approach depends to a certain extent on physical arrangements—a classroom that can be converted into a kind of laboratory setting, perhaps with movable tables and chairs that can be arranged to accommodate writing or conferences or discussion. The workshop approach depends also on the seriousness of the students because basically it encourages students to teach themselves. Workshops are ideal for teaching writing, but a teacher first has to believe in the approach and then know how to make it work.

7

Topics

Assigning topics for writing is one of the most important things a composition teacher does. In fact, topics can make the difference between an exciting class and a routine one for both students and teacher alike. I must be quite frank: I will not give certain topics to freshman students because I don't want to read what I know they will write on subjects like their most exciting moment in high school or why they are coming to college. Topics like these invite the worst possible clichés. They are not springboards for writing; they are traps. They don't give students a chance to reveal that they can think inventively.

There are several criteria that a good topic ought to meet.

1. *A good topic ought to have a purpose.*

Certain topics have a purpose only in the context of the course; that is, they may be designed to elicit a particular kind of writing from students. The purpose may be to write a persuasive argument or strike a meaningful analogy or develop a contrast. One of the silliest topics I can think of is to ask someone to describe tying a tie. If the writer's purpose is to teach someone how to tie a tie, then two or three illustrations or a short demonstration will be more efficient than 300 words. If the teacher's purpose is to teach students how to write clear directions, then the subject ought to lend itself to words. It is better not to write about some things.

2. *A good topic ought to be meaningful within the student's experience.*

A meaningful topic doesn't necessarily mean one that is personal, although it should prompt some involvement. Despite the assumption among many teachers that students want to write only about themselves, I have found almost the opposite to be true. Unless the teacher-student relationship is wholly compatible, great numbers of students can be very guarded about expressing personal feelings and preferences because they are not sure what reception they will get. They don't want to be vulnerable. They will avoid scorn if they can. Furthermore, they make a distinction between the kinds of things they will talk about in the dormitory and the kinds of things they will talk about in the classroom. They consider certain topics "too personal," indicating reservations about private matters and suggesting that they don't want to be subject to the peeping-Tomism of an instructor. Good topics ought to permit students to draw upon experience for example and support.

3. *A good topic ought to prefer specific and immediate situations to abstract and theoretical ones.*

It is not too difficult to imagine the difference in response one would get to a topic like "Discuss freedom" and another that reads: "List the freedoms you enjoy where you live and the freedoms you are denied. What is the reason for the denials? Do you accept the reasons? Write an essay on the subject." The first topic might elicit a theme like the second one, but it is not likely to. In a school setting, many students would think that their personal freedoms in the home or dormitory were not quite worthy of an awesome topic like freedom, all too often discussed with platitudes and bombast. An assignment should help reduce the awesomeness and remoteness that students attach to a subject and make it accessible to them in terms they can understand and write about.

4. *A good topic posing a hypothetical situation should be within a student's grasp.*

Topics that use hypothetical situations can sometimes provide an imaginative stimulus or supply a kind of channel for thoughts that would otherwise be difficult to express. Of the first variety is a topic like the following: "If you were the first chimpanzee to be landed on Mars, what message would you deliver to Earthlings?" This device is based on reversal, the same technique Swift uses in *Gulliver's Travels*. In fact, this kind of topic might be combined with readings from Swift to indicate how satire is implicit in the strategy.

Of the second order of topics that provide an indirect vehicle for personal expression, one like the following opens up a number of interesting possibilities: "Write an extended obituary notice for the newspaper upon the occasion of your own death." A topic of this kind taps all kinds of hopes and illusions about the future. Does one student hope to live to be ninety, have six children, twenty grandchildren, and fifty-five great-grandchildren and die as Grand Wizard of the Ku Klux Klan? And another perish at twenty-seven attempting to row solo from San Francisco to Tahiti? Although the obituary topic supposedly requires some projection into the future, it actually concerns values that a student holds at the present. This kind of hypothetical topic is quite different from one that addresses a seventeen-year-old by saying, "If you were an old man or woman . . . ." If the purpose is to find out what it is like to be old or how the old think, it would be far preferable to have young people talk to old people and report their impressions. Young students can also write easily enough from their own experience on a topic like the following: "A change in zoning laws will allow a McDonald's restaurant to be built within a block from your house. Write an essay on why this should or should not be allowed to happen." Their comments on the question might be revealing even to a politician.

5. A good topic ought to encourage a student to write.
The main purpose of a topic is to stimulate thought and give students a start. The topic itself should not be a barrier; that is, it should not be so complex that students are unable to read it readily and understand the implications. Although topics should be stated as more than a brief phrase, too many leads or too many instructions suggest that the teacher wants the subject developed in just one way.

A second purpose of a topic is to offer students a focus for writing, as long as that focus provides a number of possibilities for development: defend or deny; agree or disagree; choose someone from among your acquaintances to illustrate. Choice is certainly good, but limitless choice ("Write on anything you want to") usually proves self-defeating. Students flounder when supposedly they can choose anything in the world. They prefer suggestions and boundaries as long as they have some room to move around. For a theme assignment, four or five topics from which students can choose are better than only one. If I give as many as five topics, I like to include one that I call "nutty"— actually a topic, like the one about the chimpanzee on Mars, that requires a special kind of invention or humor. It gives some students a way to stretch themselves imaginatively, to use abilities that an ordinary topic would not tap: "Write an imaginary autobiography of a dill pickle." "Write an essay on why doorknobs are hairless." Most students are unable to write on topics of this kind, but those who can will welcome the chance and often do unusually well.

Having said what I think good topics ought to be, I am fully aware that it is easier to say what something should be than to produce the models. Nevertheless, I'll give a variety of topics on different subjects that I think are workable. These are designed for young people at the senior high school level or freshman year in college, although some of them might be adapted for younger ages.

Personal

Describe yourself as you think someone else (possibly a friend) would describe you to a third party.

Consider *one* of the following: (1) your present attitudes toward money, (2) your present attitudes toward death, or (3) your present attitudes toward the police. To what extent have these attitudes been shaped by personal experience, other people, movies or TV, or any other significant influence? Have you changed your ideas since your earlier youth? If so, what influenced the change?

Social

Write an essay on a particular characteristic of your generation that annoys you. Make your complaints specific.

Sports/Philosophy

Discuss the aptness of Bear Bryant's metaphor that "football is life." If you prefer, invent your own metaphor and develop it.

Film

Go to the media center and watch the 16-minute film called *The Encounter*.[1] Jot down what you think the silent actress is thinking and feeling. Watch the film again, looking for further details and evidence that will support your views. Write a composition about the thoughts and feelings of the silent actress, using the details you have accumulated. Or create a voice for the character and have her explain her own situation.

Quotation

There is an old Spanish proverb that goes: "The journey is more important than the inn." Write an essay on what this saying means to you. Illustrate from your own experience.

Practical letter

A good friend of yours has applied for a job as a receptionist in a large stockbroker's office and is required to submit a character reference. You have agreed to write a letter of recommendation. Write a letter describing your friend's better qualities so that the employer will accept your words as an honest appraisal based upon firsthand knowledge.

[1]David Campbell, dir., Perennial Education, Inc., 1971.

Song

Sometimes the lyrics of popular songs clearly lie about the way life is, and sometimes they are all too true. Briefly quote from a song that you think does one or the other and then say why, basing your explanation upon a specific experience of your own or of someone you know.

Language

People often say that those who use profanity show that they have a weak vocabulary. H. L. Mencken said that it takes talent to be a good swearer. Take a stand: Is profanity a form of tired speech or a vital part of English? Or something else?

Nature

"I went to the woods because I wished to live deliberately, to front only the essential facts of life, and see if I could learn what it had to teach," writes Thoreau of his retreat to Walden Pond. Recall your own experience of an extended contact with nature. What changes did you notice in yourself in terms of your priorities, tempo, or life style? What "facts of life," if any, did you distill from the experience?

These are all examples of discrete topics, isolated from one another and from the topics of another week. Some teachers attempt to remove what they consider the artificiality of classroom writing by establishing a thematic continuity throughout an entire quarter or semester. Thematic topics can best be pursued if the reading material has been chosen with that purpose in mind. Theme assignments, however, can be almost completely individualized if students take the matter seriously. I once attempted to let students in a class design their own topics by asking them at the end of each theme to write me a note telling me where their thinking in the present essay led them and what they wanted to pursue next as an outgrowth or offshoot of this effort. It was an attempt to set up a rhythm of assignments. To most of them, however, 500 words were dead end. Only about five of twenty-five students—and they were the best ones—were able to analyze their own thoughts in this way and pursue a linked program. The others leaned on me for suggestions. After that quarter, I gave up the idea because I seemed to be thinking *for* the students rather than helping them learn *how* to think. I ended up working much too hard. At that time, I did not know about heuristic procedures that might have helped them help themselves. I do not mean to discredit the strategy of continuing topics on the basis of my own limited experience, but anyone who undertakes it should know that it requires a vast amount of energy and ingenuity or some expertise with heuristics, discussed in the following chapter.[2]

Recent experiments with writing laboratories attached to subjects in other disciplines, sometimes called adjunct courses, have proved remarkably successful in solving the problem of motivation in writing classes. These are classes that carry their own units of credit and grade but draw all of the students from another class in which they are registered. That class may be a large lecture section in history, political science, or psychology. Students do the usual writing assignments for the lecture class. They work on these in the writing class and have additional assignments, but all of them are based on the material of the core course. Writing thus becomes a special way of mastering the material. But, of primary importance, students have a different attitude toward the way they write. They want the writing to be good because a grade is at stake in two classes—double jeopardy. Even though students are doing academic writing in both courses, the writing suddenly seems to have a "real" purpose.

Since writing in the composition class always seems to be more of a simulated experience than writing in other classes, teachers need to seek constantly to find ways to make the writing purposive. It is one of the justifications for writing about literature, as long as the teacher does not forget to teach writing. The caution is necessary, because neglecting the writing is all too common when literature is included. The two, however,

---

[2]For a positive, detailed description of a semester's work with continuing topics, I highly recommend *The Plural I* by William E. Coles, Jr. (New York: Holt, Rinehart and Winston, 1978).

complement one another beautifully if the teacher thinks of the two focuses—reading and writing—as equally important.

Further, to keep motivation high, teachers have to be alert to timely topics—current events, campus activities, human-interest stories in the newspaper, films, new books. These should become ways to enlarge the context of the students' experience. They should always be ways to allow them to discover new insights.

A few words need to be said about the specifications of an assignment: the length, the purpose, the mode, the audience. The less such things need to be rehearsed, the more natural writing in a classroom will become. It should be understood early in the course that most themes will be about 400-500 words—or whatever the specified length is—but counting is unnecessary. The merit of an essay will rest on its development and completeness, and 500 words ultimately becomes a very short space for an experienced writer. How long should an in-class theme be? Fifty minutes' worth (if that is the length of the class). From a purely practical standpoint, students ought to be able to write from 350 to 500 words in 50 minutes. If they can't, then they are likely to be in trouble writing examinations in their other classes. And who will be the audience? Unless otherwise specified, it will be their peers. But almost all students realize that their peers do not read their papers. Realistically, as most of them know, the teacher is the only audience.

In most instances, the purpose, mode, and audience will be implicit in the nature and wording of the topic. If a topic begins, "Re-create in essay form an experience that led you to some perception about yourself," we have a topic that naturally invites narration. If another topic begins, "Comment upon a particularly sexist attitude or practice that annoys you," we open up the possibility of definition. Topics that basically ask "Why?" invite explanation, perhaps argumentation. Teachers should try to emphasize that the mode of writing shifts naturally as we turn from one kind of question to another. "What happened?" produces narration. "Where did it happen?" invites description. An apt selection of topics can result in a series of assignments that will familiarize students with different forms. Whenever possible, teachers should try to encourage students to let their intuitions lead them into natural patterns of expression. Writing will then become less a matter of fulfilling an assignment or doing what "the teacher wants." Mode will be related to purpose.

The deadline is usually the other crucial specification in academic writing. Deadlines are not bad as long as the time between an assignment and the due date allows for an incubation period—a time for brewing. Ideally, students should have at least one week to prepare, write, and revise a paper. The fact that most of them may write their papers the night before the due date does not mean that the other six days have been wasted. Great numbers of writers wait for the pressure of a deadline to get around to putting words on paper. In the interim, their topic has alerted them, either consciously or subconsciously, to material they can use. The pre-writing period is never lost time.

Pre-Writing

Pre-writing refers to the time before writing begins in a formal sense, but it does not mean a period of "no writing." During pre-writing, writers may do various kinds of informal scribbling—making lists, jotting down thoughts, keeping a journal, or outlining. The pre-writing period ought to be a time of exploration—observing and recording perceptions. Despite the fact that much of the data that is gathered may be discarded, the act of collecting makes possible associations that may not have otherwise occurred to the writer. The pre-writing period is the primary generative stage of writing. For that reason, it is not a stage that we master at some point and pass through. Pre-writing is a necessary pre-condition of writing.

What needs to be asked here is what part the instructor can have in this period of personal and private gathering and reflection. The simple answer is that the instructor can help students develop pre-writing skills that make the job of writing easier. I think of these in two categories: first, activities that help students loosen up and overcome the psychological barriers to writing and, second, those that help students see the importance of structural paradigms as ways of generating ideas. One category suggests freedom; the other, control. But, paradoxically, the two work to support each other in the thinking process. Let me explain.

By the time students have gone through the school system, most of them have learned that they are expected to give organized responses to questions, that is, answers that are relevant, pointed, and accurate. Answering a question is an occasion for focus, not scanning. Answering a question is getting to the point, not skirting it. Answering a question is coupling the mind to an issue and dealing with it. Mind you, all students don't do these things, but most of them know they are supposed to.

The need for directness in answering questions poses a difficulty for many students when we in the English classroom ask them to discuss, that is, to be discursive. Many of them seek the same kind of linear direction that exists between a single question and a correct answer. And that kind of single-directedness does not allow the mind to play, to associate, to discover, to formulate. By the time students reach a mature stage of mental development, they often have to relearn the importance of free and spontaneous exploration. They have to learn that searching for ideas, especially new ones or new perspectives on old ideas, is considering multiple possibilities before focusing; letting the mind see relations before discovering. No doubt, every inventor has left behind a mass of discarded ideas before settling upon a solution. That is the true nature of the generative process, not asking one question and answering it, but considering many and letting the answers reveal themselves.

I have been trying to characterize what I think of as a kind of mental up-tightness in many students. I am not decrying whatever training they have had in mental discipline intended to allow them to respond relevantly, pointedly, and accurately to questions, but I am saying that many of them need mental gymnastics before they can free themselves to think agilely. The pre-writing emphasis in the classroom can provide those kinds of limbering up exercises.

For a number of years, I have asked students in my class on "The Composition Process" to make a collage on a subject of their choice. I encourage them not to decide first what they want to do or say in this visual medium, but if it is at all possible simply to collect as many pictures as possible in an indiscriminate way and then let the pictures suggest a selection and arrangement for a finished product.

I ask them to do two additional things: keep a journal listing the steps they went through from the time of the assignment to completing the collage, making clear what decisions went into the composition and indicating the degree of their satisfaction or frustration with what they have done. And, second, attempt to say in words what the pictures say collectively, not by telling what the collage is *about*, but by trying to make an equivalent verbal statement. They can write a prose statement, a poem, or a story, whatever permits them to parallel the collage as closely as possible.

The assignment turns out to be especially interesting during the summer quarter when I have a number of experienced teachers with teenage children. Sometimes they get considerable ribbing from their children about cutting out pictures and playing around with them. But even that mockery has its purpose because it suggests that serious matters do not always have to appear to be serious. Making a collage is fun; it seems not to be a serious matter.

Let me briefly list some of the typical findings as a result of this assignment.

1. Some individuals are incapable of relinquishing control of their thoughts to the extent that they are able to collect pictures first and then let the pictures decide the theme. Anyone who determines a theme or thesis first and then looks for pictures to fit has trouble, because inevitably the exact illustrations aren't always available. Some individuals are almost incapable of free exploration. Those who pursue it eagerly, perhaps for the first time, are pleased with the results, despite the fact that they end up with a mass of rejected material.

2. Freedom of exploration does not mean total freedom for anyone. The magazines someone has available almost immediately begin to narrow the possible range of subjects. *Woman's Day* obviously produces a different assemblage of pictures than *National Geographic.* Some people decide early along the way that they want all colored pictures. Others have to eliminate pictures that are too big or too small. All of the various constraints and preliminary decisions become immensely important when one begins to realize how they shape the final product.

3. Many students discover that they cannot begin to say in a traditional prose statement, linear in character, what the multi-dimensional, nonlinear collage says. Some of them for the first time in their lives write a poem and are pleased that they can. The freedom of exploration has led them to find a new form for what they want to say.

4. The journals suggest over and over again that zeroing in too soon on a thesis gets students boxed in. At that point, they have to start over or face further frustrations. Openness as long as possible facilitates the process and constantly keeps open the possibility of new arrangements. The decisions that occur are basically intuitive or aesthetic. Anyone who plans the juxtapositions of certain pictures to mean something quite precise is surprised to find that colleagues often do not catch the intended meaning, but see others that have not occurred to the maker.

5. Making a collage becomes a correlative of the writing process, revealing to many individuals essentially why their unwillingness to let the mind scan limits their capacities for expression. The search for ideas cannot always be deliberate. Ideas emerge, despite the constraints that affect each of us in a particular situation.

Various kinds of free-writing exercises in the classroom are often valuable as means of overcoming psychological barriers to writing and as ways of discovering, sometimes with surprise, what the mind in a state of relatively free association can come up with.

For students who have had little practice in writing, it is a good idea to devote 5 or 10 minutes at the beginning of each period to "free" writing. Basically, "free" means free of the usual criticism, editing, and grading, although students ought to write in a notebook so that they have an accumulation of their own ideas after a period of time.

In the beginning, the exercise can take the form of "wet-ink" writing, having students force themselves to continue writing for five minutes without taking pen from paper. If nothing occurs to them, let them write, "I can't think of anything to write. I can't think of anything to write." Something will occur to them after two or three sentences of that kind. Wet-ink writing is important as a means of overcoming blank-paper paralysis. Words go down on paper. That's the important beginning.

On home assignments, students who suffer from the procrastination syndrome or the perfectionist complex should be encouraged to set an alarm clock for 60 or 75 minutes and then write as rapidly as possible to get down a rough draft before the alarm sounds. They are often pleasantly surprised that what they have written is usable and frequently much more polished than they would have expected. I have come to the conclusion that in-class essays are often more readable than out-of-class papers for the simple reason that students have not had time to overwork them.

To vary the format of wet-ink writing, the instructor can encourage observation or free association of ideas by playing a record (preferably a selection without words), bringing to class a picture or a piece of sculpture, or showing a short film. Again, the emphasis should be upon free expression, not finished products. Always in this kind of writing there should be some pushing of the mind and imagination. Instead of saying "Describe what you see," say "List thirty-five details." Unusual, unfamiliar music provides a better imaginative stimulus than familiar lyric compositions. I have had good luck with parts of Karlheinz Stockhausen's *Momente* and John Cage's *Variations*.

A free-writing period at the beginning of each hour for three or four weeks has two particularly worthwhile effects. It creates the expectation that writing classes are places where people come to write, and it makes writing habitual. Thinking of the composition class as a workshop has merit. Students can work at their own pace and consult with the instructor when they need to. The writing requirement can even be worked out on a contract basis if the instructor wants to individualize the work further. Many such efforts, however, prove to be more complicated than rewarding. And there are advantages in having everyone writing on a common topic if the instructor wants to compare differences in treatment. Let me illustrate.

Upon occasion, I have shown a short, 9-minute film entitled *The Dot and the Line*.[1] Actually it is a film produced for mathematics instruction. Its abstractions, however, make it a good departure for a short writing assignment. The film lends itself to a number of different interpretations. After the students view the film, I ask them simply to write down what it said to them. I emphasize that I am interested in what they see, not what they think they are supposed to see. Here are three statements, typical of most of the others:

> 1. I found myself relating the dot, line, and squiggle to people. The line and squiggle are men, one the straight and narrow, boring type and the other a wild, freaky guy. The dot reminded me of a good-looking girl who was infatuated with the wild squiggle because she could be wild and crazy and always have a good time with him. [The narrative continues, telling how Straight-line's work paid off because in the end he used what he had learned to be creative and interesting.]

> 2. In this short film, the line seems to point out a few factors to me. The line represented conformity, conservatism, and the act of doing things in the same pattern consistently. To me, the line seemed to be saying experiment, open your mind to let your thoughts run freely. If you let yourself go and have confidence in what *you* as an individual have to work with, you may experience things that you'd never thought were possible. This was illustrated when the line decided to try something new and consequently the dot liked and appreciated him. If people weren't so inhibited and afraid to let themselves go, many more things would be created and tried. If you have confidence in yourself that you can be creative and produce something worthwhile, then per-

---

[1] Metro-Goldwyn-Mayer, 1965.

haps more people would open up and experiment with the ideals that life has to offer.

3. The film was trying to show the aspect of a line people seldom think about. When one speaks of a line, we usually think of something that is straight with only one dimension. However, by the bending of a line, forms of two and three dimensions can be formed. Curves can be made with straight edge and pencil. With practice even circles can be formed in the same manner. Many of the intricate designs shown can be made with pencil and straight edge. The film also brought out the importance of lines in areas of concern to many. In art, lines form the edges of objects to show the demarcation between the object and the background. In sports, the line marks out certain areas on a field of play. Football and baseball require lines for proper control of play. In politics, boundaries (lines) are important to mark off each country's territory. There's more to a line than just being straight. Lines are present in our views. Lines are important.

The pieces were written in 15 minutes without any time for preparation and were turned in without revision so that I could ditto several selections and use them as the basis for discussion at the next class session. Any English teacher could edit each of these selections with relish if that were the object. The purpose, however, was to show differences in approach and response to the same film.

At least one-third of the students took the first approach. It equates the situation in the film depicting mathematical forms with life experience. The forms are people. They interact. These students see a story with a moral. The moral varies slightly from person to person, but it has to do with the triumph of love or of hard work or of sound values. Almost anyone viewing the film can make this kind of human equation. It is the most obvious interpretation.

The second writer certainly does not ignore the story line, but the forms are not an "old boyfriend I used to have" or "the guy hung up on drugs." The forms are primarily symbolic. The film is a short disquisition on strict conformity and flexibility. At least half of the class treated the film similarly. They observed the difference between order and anarchy or reason and irrationality. In almost all instances, talking about qualities eliminated the element of narrative characteristic of the experience approach.

The third writer, typical of one-sixth of the group, does essentially what the second writer did, but tries to treat "the aspect of a line people seldom think about." This writer manages to tap new resources of thought by shifting away from the immediate situation of the film and thinking about lines in other contexts—or considering what Kenneth Pike calls their "distribution in larger contexts."[2]

I would of course want students to observe these differences themselves. I think they need to discover that what is obvious to everyone doesn't inform the reader to any great extent. "In other words," writes James Kinneavy, "the 'information' in a statement consists in the degree of improbability of a statement."[3] The samples on *The Dot and the Line* illustrate for the group what is the most probable and how it is possible to get beyond the obvious, not by thinking harder, but by thinking in other contexts.

Class discussion can also be characterized as a pre-writing activity. Its purpose is to overcome the passivity of students and get them to act and interact. I don't have to argue the virtues of discussion. Both students and teachers consistently seem to want it. Yet, if I can judge accurately from the thousands of student surveys I have read during the last ten years, the efforts of teachers to get discussions going are often in vain. Students say this. And the teachers tell me the same thing. From time to time, I discover a rare teacher who can lead a discussion the way everybody wants a discussion to go. That's when I try to learn how it's done.

The secret is not absolutely astounding: the people who are best at leading a discussion are best at keeping their own mouths shut. We don't have to go much further to say why most teachers are unsuccessful in leading discussions. They *can't* keep their mouths shut. In fact, they think they are not doing their jobs unless they are talking. Then there is also the incontrovertible fact that most of us cannot bear silence during

---

[2]Richard E. Young, Alton L. Becker, and Kenneth L. Pike, *Rhetoric: Discovery and Change* (New York: Harcourt, Brace & World, 1970), p. 56.
[3]*A Theory of Discourse* (Englewood Cliffs, N.J.: Prentice-Hall, Inc., 1971), p. 93.

a discussion. If no one says anything immediately, we fill in. At best, the teacher's role in a discussion is to orchestrate—to take what is given and try to make a coherent whole of it. The teacher should try to keep some kind of control so that discussions do not degenerate into bull sessions. A teacher may expand and develop a student's comment, but for the most part cannot correct it or by irony expose it as stupid. I can remember clearly one of my graduate professors who used to irritate me because he would never counter a remark made in class, no matter how wrongheaded it was. I'm sure I was at that time committed to the view that ignorance and stupidity had to be openly flouted and purged. I don't know exactly when I changed my mind—many years later, I'm sure—but I am now more certain of two things. If I squelch one student, that student and a dozen others are not likely to participate again. If I let something stupid go by the way without comment, I don't have to worry too much. Stupidities have a remarkable way of filtering out and dissolving. Now some thirty years after the seminar I referred to, I do not remember any of the wrong things that were said, but I do remember that it was a stimulating seminar and discussion always went well. Further, I still remember the professor with respect and affection. His tolerance did not compromise his standards of excellence.

Leading a discussion is directly related to the teacher-student relationship we talked about in Chapter 5. Teachers who are intimidating and dogmatic are not likely to be good discussion leaders. Further, questions and answers do not substitute for discussion. If discussion is only horizontal—student talking to teacher and teacher replying to student—not much interaction occurs among other students. The best discussions are lateral—student to student, back and forth. For this reason, many teachers think that the typical grid classroom militates against a good discussion. That is true to a certain extent, but moving chairs in a circle doesn't insure a good discussion. It only provides a more appropriate setting.

Much of the difficulty in discussion technique begins with the "starter." Many teachers think they are inviting free and open discussion if they begin by saying as informally as possible,

"Well, what did you think of the essay we read?" or "Did you like it?" These are both dead-end questions, because students know that the teacher is not interested in hearing someone say the essay was dreary and dated. It's undoubtedly supposed to be "interesting," or the anthologist wouldn't have chosen it and the teacher wouldn't have chosen the anthology. So they go along with those questions and say what they're supposed to say in order to get past that hurdle.

The best starter for a good discussion is the truly open question. I would define the open question, not as one to which there is no single answer, but as one to which the teacher has no single answer. One of the most common student complaints about teachers they don't like is that those teachers do not entertain opinions different from their own. What I sometimes find distressing is that the most intolerant teachers somehow imagine themselves as remarkably receptive and then wonder why discussions don't go well. Discussions cannot be exercises in clairvoyance—everyone trying to say what the teacher is thinking. Students usually know when the "right" thing has been said, because openness to further comment seems to end and the teacher monopolizes the discussion.

One other pre-writing strategy depends strongly for its success upon the students' attitude toward it. That is the use of the journal. Keeping journals became popular in the late '60s. Students are now asked to write journal entries not only in composition classes but in literature classes as well. The popularity of the journal somewhat defeats its purpose as a record of the individual's intellectual and emotional responses to ideas and experiences. The journal is supposed to provide the student with an outlet for thoughts that are not going to be censured for one reason or another; it is supposed to allow the student to experiment, to try something new. If students become facile at writing journal entries, filling up pages the day before journals are due because they have to turn something in, then the journal becomes a sham.

Those teachers who believe in the value of journals or those who want to determine what those values are ought to keep several things in mind.

1. Writing in a journal is a pre-writing activity. Yet most students are not going to take a journal seriously unless it "counts." That means it has to fulfill some portion of the writing requirement in the course. On this basis, keeping a journal can be made optional. A journal kept for four weeks can count for three themes or some percentage of the total requirement. Students who don't want to bother with a journal can meet the requirement in the usual way. Students who keep a journal ought to do so willingly and know its purpose as a generative device. No one should be penalized for either keeping or not keeping a journal.

2. Journals should be read but by no means graded. Some instructors don't want to tamper at all with the thoughts recorded in the journal. I am inclined to think that teachers lose an opportunity to cash in on the journal if they do not react to the best that is there. Marginal comments ought to encourage students to continue in a particular direction: "What you write here comes out clearly and naturally" (a comment on voice); "A good idea that you could use as the basis for a theme" (reaction to a striking thought); "This is the kind of experience that makes a good illustration" (an attempt to make some discrimination by identifying the best); "I like this" (honest praise, but only when the instructor means it).

3. Journals should be abandoned after three or four weeks unless a student wants to continue voluntarily. This suggestion is based on the assumption that several weeks is adequate to demonstrate the value of the journal. If it is sufficiently helpful to someone, that person will continue. Others who have been doing the journals perfunctorily will derive no new benefits by being forced to continue for a full quarter or semester. In short, journals are a teaching strategy whose worth, like all strategies, should be determined by the results it gets.

.   .   .

The second category of pre-writing activities is based upon the theory that we can assist the generative process of the mind by applying systematic procedures. A systematic approach helps the memory retrieve material relevant to the investigation at hand; it encourages discovery; and it insures a more thorough investigation than we are likely to accomplish by chance inquiry. Further, structured investigation tends to activate intuitive perceptions by setting up relationships between things which we otherwise tend to see as isolated fragments.

In the teaching of composition, we have almost always assumed in the past that intelligent people could generate ideas; our job as teachers was to help them express ideas effectively. Of course, intelligent people can generate ideas, but that doesn't mean they cannot profit from a systematic procedure, as long as that approach does not mechanize their thinking. What is formulaic about a system must remain flexible. What is structured must correspond closely to the way the minds of most people work. Thus it is possible to invent algorithms, paradigms, rubrics—whatever one wants to call them—to aid our thinking.

Upon many occasions, I have heard composition teachers say that the aim of their course is to teach students how to think. I have never taken their comments too seriously because "how to think" usually means "*what* to think." Certainly intellectual stimulation is an important pre-writing activity, but it has nothing to do with thinking in a formal sense, like testing syllogisms, detecting fallacies, tracing the development of a thesis, or with the kind of systematic investigation that is now often referred to as heuristic procedure. Teachers interested in teaching students *how* to think can actually do so by demonstrating how a system works and how an organized approach can produce better thinking and writing. Teachers unfamiliar with a generative system will not be persuaded of the value of heuristics until they have actually worked with one themselves. It is important to have the firsthand experience in order to anticipate the kind of problems that can arise.

We cannot explain here the full implications of a particular device, but two brief descriptions will indicate the nature of a heuristic procedure. Two conditions are important for any scheme. First, it must be relatively simple so that we can keep it readily in mind to summon when we want to. If the algorithm is a series of questions, the limit should be five to seven, certainly not more than nine, for the mind does not readily retain more categories than that.[4] Schemes that attempt an all-inclusiveness by listing twenty or twenty-five questions are useless because we have difficulty retaining extended lists. The second important condition is that the terms must be blanket terms. They cannot be limited to one particular subject. They must apply generally to any subject.

The following four-part heuristic is adapted from Kenneth Pike's use of particle-wave-field theory from physics as the basis of varying the ways we can view experience. It is a controlled device for changing perspective and thus for generating thoughts that may not have occurred to us without the use of this algorithm:

1. Consider an object or experience as an individual, self-contained unit (a tree, a building, a person);
2. Consider it as it relates to the things immediately around it (a variation of 1, inviting comparison or contrast);
3. Consider it over a period of time (changing, maturing, dying);
4. Consider it as part of a larger context or system (historically, sociologically, aesthetically).[5]

This scheme suggests a series of concentric circles, ever-widening contexts in which to consider an object or experience.

Kenneth Burke uses a different metaphor. He calls it his dramatistic method. In simplest terms, it applies the language of drama to any experience involving motives:

Action—What is happening?
Agent—Who is doing it?

---

[4]George A. Miller, "The Magical Number Seven, Plus or Minus Two: Some Limits on Our Capacity for Processing Information," *The Psychological Review,* 63 (1956), 81-97. A later article by Donald E. Broadbent includes data that suggest the constant number is nearer five than seven ("The Magic Number Seven After Fifteen Years" in *Studies in Long Term Memory,* eds. Alan Kennedy and Alan Wilkes [London: John Wiley, 1975], pp. 3-18).

[5]For a more extended treatment of this heuristic procedure, see Young, Becker, and Pike, pp. 126-130.

Agency—How is it being done?
Scene—Where and when?
Purpose—Why?

The five questions are of course familiar to all journalists. Emphasis should be placed, however, on the total conception of something as a drama involving actors acting in a particular setting with varying purposes. It is not difficult to see that these basic questions can be altered and expanded by altering the terms. "What was happening?" investigates the past. "What will happen?" makes conjectures about the future. The negative form of each question opens further channels of thought. "Who is *not* doing it [smoking marijuana]?" may be as illuminating in an investigation of the subject as the positive question. Burke's pentad helps us to see experience as if it were a total drama. As Pike's scheme also reveals, experience can be perceived as if it were isolated and static, but it can also be viewed as dynamic, contributing to larger systems. These algorithms keep the mind tuned to new channels and thus to variations of our most set ways of thinking.

Burke's pentad is also useful to help students generate a series of related papers. Having selected a general topic, a student can write a Who-paper, a What-paper, a How-paper, etc. One of the most impressive series I ever received was written by a young woman, who at the beginning of the quarter said she wanted to write on Judaism. Her Who-paper was a masterful series of character sketches of five married couples, all of whom claimed to be Jewish, but were completely different in their beliefs and life styles. That was her answer to "Who Is a Jew?" Her How-paper was an exposition of orthodox Jewish customs and rituals. Her Where-and-When-paper was a description of life in an Israeli kibbutz. She completed the series with a What-paper and a Why-paper. Another student did a series on chess. He wasn't a particularly good student, but he wrote a fascinating set of papers extending from "Who's Who in Chess" to "Why People Like to Play Chess." He had a subject he was deeply involved in. The heuristic procedure gave him a means to explore and focus.

For the general background on various approaches, Richard Young's chapter on "Invention: A Topographical Survey" in *Teaching Composition: Ten Bibliographical Essays* is an indispensable source.[6] Chapter 4 of my own book *The Holt Guide to English* contains an extended description of the use of Kenneth Burke's pentad,[7] demonstrating how a teacher can lead students through the questions until they can apply the technique themselves. Chapter 3 of Ross Winterowd's *The Contemporary Writer*[8] covers three heuristic procedures, including the tagmemic scheme originated by Kenneth Pike and treated extensively in several chapters of *Rhetoric: Discovery and Change,* already referred to.

REPRESENTATIVE PROJECTS

1. Using the paradigm on p. 90, have students describe an object four separate times, changing the perspective each time as the paradigm indicates.

2. Have students list fifty facts about an event or series of events they have experienced or read about. Have them use Burke's pentad to generate details about characters, actions, setting, etc. At the end of the list, have them write two points they can make by describing this event. The next step is to have them write the description.

3. Think through a topic with a class by recording their observations in brief notes on the board. Begin with a broad topic like "Marijuana should/should not be legalized" or "Euthanasia should/should not be allowed" or "Transcendental Meditation can/cannot save the human race." See what patterns emerge. Are the arguments personal (pertaining to the Actor)? Are they social (pertaining to the Scene)? Are they moral (pertaining to the Purpose)?

[6]Ed. Gary Tate (Fort Worth, Texas: Texas Christian University Press, 1976).
[7](2nd ed., New York: Holt, Rinehart and Winston, 1976).
[8](New York: Harcourt Brace Jovanovich, 1975).

Do they concern means of implementation (Agency)? Do they concern interpretation of what precisely is meant (the nature of the Action)? Or do different kinds of patterns emerge altogether? In short, try to distill from the discussion a paradigm that satisfies the class and that they might find applicable to other issues.

4. Use the familiar communications triangle as the basis for a heuristic: writer, message, and reader—these considered in a context that might be labeled "situation." Then, have the class formulate questions:

> What kinds of questions can be asked about the writer on the basis of a written sample?
> What kinds of questions can be asked about the message or arguments?
> What kinds of questions can be asked about the reader/audience and their relation to the writer and the mode of the message?
> What kinds of questions can be asked about the situation from which this message emerges and which has possibly influenced it?

5. Have students equate camera and film techniques with comparable writing techniques: long-shot, full shot, close-up, flashback, scan, montage, internal rhythm, external rhythm, measurable time reversal, spatial continuity, spatial discontinuity. The parallels will lead immediately to considerations of form and development.

9

Teaching Structure

In the previous chapter, we were concerned with generating ideas, what in classical rhetoric was classified as *inventio*. This chapter treats what in classical rhetoric was called *dispositio* or arrangement. In contemporary terms, if the previous chapter was concerned with generating content, then this one is concerned with the shape of content. If invention pertains to acquiring knowledge, arrangement pertains to modifying it for a particular purpose. The situation of writing may well determine the degree of conventionality or innovation that is suitable. Even though we may make a separation of pre-writing and arrangement for purposes of teaching, we should not think of them as separate and discrete stages in practice.

Many students find pre-writing exercises painful because they have not learned to cope with chaos—or what appears to be chaos. They don't want to range freely; they don't want to collect and generate material they are not going to use. They are not willing to accept the basic truth of the opening of Chapter 82 of Melville's *Moby-Dick*: "There are some enterprises in which a careful disorderliness is the true method." They would rather be orderly from the start, ignoring the fact that it is wholly possible to get oneself boxed in too soon so that the full implications of a topic remain unexplored. There are strong reasons to recommend that writers *not* map out a precise itinerary too soon. They need to have a direction, to be sure, but not an exact plan. It is not wholly metaphorical to say that we find form as we write. Theme and content suggest a shape as writing begins and continues. Out of the material, a "conceptual map" takes shape.[1] Discoveries of new ideas along the way can alter the direction we take or change the proportions of our presentation.

The phrase "the shape of content" I have used belongs to Ben Shahn. It is the title of one of the lectures (and a subsequent book) he delivered at Harvard in 1956-1957 when he spoke of the demands that form makes upon the artist.[2] Form is both a selector and shaper; finding form is a process of discovery, not just applying a set pattern to available material. In his lecture, Shahn considers six conditions for finding form:

1. Determining a theme
2. Gathering material [the collage exercise suggests that No. 1 and No. 2 may be interchangeable]
3. Setting limits, what Shahn calls an "outer shape"
4. Relating the inner parts to the outside limits
5. Eliminating material that does not fall within the bounds
6. Ordering the whole to meet the needs of content[3]

Content comes first, form follows—thus, what Shahn calls the shape of content. If we apply these conditions to the writing process, two terms may need some explanation: "outer shape" and the "inner parts."

When anyone mentions structure, we characteristically tend to think of shape—the outside configuration. It is a normal tendency. With more conscious effort, we come to realize that

---

[1]Mina Shaughnessy, *Errors and Expectations* (New York: Oxford University Press, 1977), p. 249.
[2]*The Shape of Content* (Cambridge: Harvard University Press, 1957).
[3]Shahn, p. 70.

almost every external shape has some kind of internal structure that supports and maintains the outward form. Thus, as we view the human body, the intricate skeletal frame is not visible, but it is the inner structure. In most buildings, the joists and supports are hidden, but they too are the structural frame. Similarly, the outer shape of written prose is obvious, but the internal supports are less apparent. Traditional teaching has given almost all of its attention to the organization of the total form rather than to the interlinking of parts. The two, of course, work in conjunction with one another, like brick and mortar, to accomplish a design.

The "outer shape" of writing, it seems to me, can be made almost wholly a prescriptive matter if a teacher chooses that approach, and many do as a way of ensuring a semblance of organization, whether or not that arrangement is the shape of the writer's thoughts. One of the most definable and teachable of the set patterns of organization, for example, is the five-paragraph theme, the first paragraph of which is the Introduction and the final one the Conclusion.

It has always puzzled me why teachers insist upon this particular form. I sometimes wonder why they require the five-paragraph theme. Of course, it may help some students structure their essays. But why the arbitrary five? Why not four? Or three? And why does no professional writer indulge in this practice? Must we acknowledge that the 500-word theme with five paragraphs is a genre peculiar to the English classroom? Some text writers seem to tell us it is and, for that reason, conclude that theme writing is necessarily divorced from any standard for writing outside the English classroom.

The five-paragraph theme undoubtedly has its origins in the form of the classical oration for argumentative discourse, the first section of which was the *exordium*, the equivalent of an Introduction, and the last section the *peroratio*, the equivalent of a Conclusion. Both terms had considerably more breadth and purpose than we attribute to Introductions and Conclusions today. The other parts had designated purposes also, but they seem to have been lost when the five-part structure was applied to other than argumentative discourse.

It is difficult to deny that the five-part essay is teachable and may even be helpful to students who are not ready to shape their own thoughts. But it is limited in its application (how many topics fall into five parts?), and it almost inevitably encourages dull, formulaic writing. For the writer, there are no discoveries. For the reader, there is no anticipation, no surprise. Much work-a-day prose of a business or technical nature has stipulated forms. But forms of that variety have a service function, like a box to put things in, not a design that together with the material expresses meaning. Flexible arrangements, of course, have to have a discernible structure, but it need not be set or predetermined. Characteristically, good writers shape their own prose. To limit the process of finding form too severely is to limit the development of students as self-sufficient writers.

The "outer shape," as Shahn calls it, need not therefore be conceived in terms of a formula—a specified number of paragraphs or paragraphs with designated purposes. The outer shape is the setting of limits that will define the whole—where the subject will begin, where it will end. Beginning does not necessarily have anything to do with an introductory paragraph or ending with a concluding one. The function of a good beginning—involving the reader—might be served by one sentence. An ending might be one paragraph or three. In brief, the structure of the whole—the intuitive perception of limits—has nothing directly to do with paragraphing. A whole with an appropriate beginning, middle, and end might consist of two paragraphs or ten, depending upon the writer's subject and purpose. Paragraphing, however, is basic to the "inner parts" that Shahn speaks of and to the ways those parts are fused to accomplish the qualities of unity and coherence that we usually associate with clear, readable writing.

The paragraph, like the composition as a whole, has been taught formulaically. It is described essentially as a form beginning with a topic sentence that sets limited boundaries for discussion, followed by exploration of that thought within those bounds. This kind of paragraph is essentially a self-contained unit. We have all read paragraphs of this variety; we have all written them. But they do not represent all paragraphs. In fact, if we accept Richard Braddock's findings, only 13 percent of expository paragraphs written by contemporary professional writers begin with topic sentences.[4]

In what other terms can we think of paragraphs that will more adequately describe what we do when we paragraph? Many of the ideas that follow reflect the thinking and writing of Francis Christensen, A. L. Becker, and Paul Rodgers, whose articles in *CCC* during 1965 and 1966 represented some of the first serious reconsideration of paragraph structure in almost a century.[5] What these men say about paragraph development also becomes basic to the construction of the essay as a whole, not in the sense that the paragraph is a microcosm of the whole, but in the sense that the generative process that prompts us to paragraph also serves to produce whole essays. Thus, in speaking of paragraphing, they open up new possibilities for explaining how we order the whole without reference to set models.

I would like to begin with Paul Rodgers, because he more than the others establishes an intuitive basis for paragraphing that can be explained in terms of the sense of closure we have discussed in Chapter 4. Rodgers reminds us that often we do not consciously construct paragraphs. We discover them. We may be more aware of the fact that we have come to the end of something (our sense of closure) than we are aware that we want to start something new. Paragraphing is placing an interpretation upon material. It is therefore like punctuation. In Rodgers' own words, "Paragraphs are not composed; they are discovered. To compose is to create; to indent is to interpret."[6]

---

[4]"The Frequency and Placement of Topic Sentences in Expository Prose," *Research in the Teaching of English*, 8 (1974), 301. Part of the problem is determining exactly what a topic sentence is. Braddock himself faced this dilemma, as he discusses in the article. I have had my graduate students try to verify Braddock's findings. Their studies indicate that percentages vary greatly among individual writers; an overall average, however, is more likely to be closer to 40 percent or 50 percent than 13 percent.

[5]For a collection of these articles, see *The Sentence and the Paragraph* (Champaign, Ill.: National Council of Teachers of English, n.d.).

[6]*The Sentence and the Paragraph*, p. 43.

In order to interpret our own material by means of paragraphing, we need the conception of outer shape or outside limits that Shahn speaks of. Then we make choices to reveal it. We paragraph in terms of a total conception we have in mind, but the totality materializes only as we create the paragraphs. Parts are known by the whole, but the whole becomes known only through the parts, just as one cannot know the meaning of a sentence without reading the words, but cannot know the exact meaning of the words without the context of the sentence. There is constant interaction of parts and whole. Composing, therefore, is not as simple as outlining and fleshing out the subtopics with prose or simply adding up parts to make a whole. Rodgers' approach to arrangement means that we have to worry little about blueprints. It means that we discover as we write; it means that the writer writes more like a sculptor who finds form while sculpting than like a bricklayer who piles bricks to construct a wall. Neither the sculptor nor the writer improvises offhandedly. Each begins with a sketch—the outer limits. Finding form is a relating of inner parts to those limits.

In Rodgers' article on the paragraph and in a subsequent one, he discusses a unit of the language he calls the stadium of discourse.[7] A stadium is a pattern of prose discourse that can be coterminous with a paragraph, smaller than a paragraph, or a combination of several paragraphs. Indentation is the means writers use to designate how they wish the patterns to be combined or separated. A reader seeing a particular passage printed without paragraphing might choose different indentation from the original writer, but the new choices would almost always correspond to subordinate patterns. For instance, Alton Becker uses the following passage from *Queen Victoria* as one of his illustrations; Lytton Strachey wrote it as one paragraph:

> The English Constitution—that indescribable entity—is a living thing, growing with the growth of men, and assuming ever-varying forms in accordance with the subtle and complex laws of human character. It

---

[7]"The Stadium of Discourse," *College Composition and Communication*, 18 (1967), 178-185.

is the child of wisdom and chance. The wise men of 1688 moulded it
into the shape we know, but the chance that George I could not speak
English gave it one of its essential peculiarities—the system of a Cabinet
independent of the Crown and subordinate to the Prime Minister. The
wisdom of Lord Grey saved it from petrification and set it upon the
path of democracy. Then chance intervened once more. A female sover-
eign happened to marry an able and pertinacious man, and it seemed
likely that an element which had been quiescent within it for years—the
element of irresponsible administrative power—was about to become its
predominant characteristic and change completely the direction of its
growth. But what chance gave, chance took away. The Consort perished
in his prime, and the English Constitution, dropping the dead limb with
hardly a tremor, continued its mysterious life as if he had never been.[8]

If students are asked where else Strachey *might* have indented,
almost all of them will recognize that another paragraph might
have begun with "Then chance intervened . . . ," and a smaller
number will suggest that for special effect another break might
occur before "But what chance gave . . . ." The exercise merely
confirms Rodgers' statements; three subpatterns occur in the
one paragraph. They are not accidental. The first one is clearly
joined by a series of pronouns whose antecedent is the "English
constitution" in the first sentence. The pronominal chain is broken at the end of sentence 4, and the fifth sentence begins with
the adverb "then," suggesting a new time segment. The third
pattern that many students recognize begins with "But," followed by a balanced structure "what chance gave, chance took
away," which is a wholly appropriate sentence to be given emphasis by indentation. In short, this would be an indentation
primarily for rhetorical effect.

Three indentations in the Strachey paragraph are therefore
possible. Strachey wrote them as one. Why? A careful analysis
of the thematic links, in addition to the lexical and grammatical
links, will support his choice, not as a matter of right or wrong,
but as a matter of interpretation and effect. And, one must
quickly add, his indentation of one paragraph depends also

[8] *The Sentence and the Paragraph,* p. 35.

upon the context in which it appears. A series of long paragraphs might well invite a very short one for contrast and emphasis. A series of short paragraphs might well invite a single long, reflective passage.

What experiments with paragraphing inevitably confirm is an intuitive perception of paragraph patterns that can be separated or combined in various ways. When one pattern extends beyond a single paragraph to include several other paragraphs, the result is a paragraph bloc, that is, a segment of discourse longer than the paragraph that operates as a single unit.[9] We encounter paragraph blocs constantly in the prose of established writers, but we have never had an identifying label for them. A bloc of four paragraphs might very well have one topic sentence that embraces the bloc of four as a whole. Thus, the paragraphing a writer chooses may be only one way—that writer's way—of partitioning the material. It is helpful to have students consider alternative paragraphing, for then they begin to realize what paragraphs do, how the structural divisions can affect the interpretation of a passage.

In an article entitled "The Psychological Reality of the Paragraph," Frank Koen, Alton Becker, and Richard Young report on their experiments "to assess the degree of agreement with which Ss [students] identify paragraph boundaries in unindented prose passages." In the experiments, some passages used nonsense paralogs in place of nouns, verbs, descriptive adjectives, and adverbs of manner. The authors conclude that "the paragraph is a psychologically real unit."[10] Readers recognize it by formal cues as well as by semantic cues. Basically, what Koen, Becker, and Young seem to be saying is that we acquire an imprint of paragraph patterns in our minds much as we internalize sentence patterns. If that is so, then it follows we can paragraph intuitively just as we write sentences intuitively.

---

[9]William F. Irmscher, *The Holt Guide to English* (2nd ed., New York: Holt, Rinehart, and Winston, 1976), pp. 99–101.

[10]*Journal of Verbal Learning and Verbal Behavior*, 8 (1969), 51.

In another article entitled "A Tagmemic Approach to Paragraph Analysis," Alton Becker identifies two major paragraph patterns.[11] The first he calls TRI, where T is essentially the topic slot; R, a restatement or expansion; and I, illustration, which can be filled by various examples or other kinds of support. R is an optional slot, so that one might recognize only TI. The slots are also reversible; thus, inductive paragraphs might be patterned as ITR or IT. A pattern such as $TRIT_1$ describes a familiar kind of paragraph that in the final sentence repeats the topic at the beginning.

The second major pattern Becker describes is PS (problem/solution), which might in many instances take the form of QA (question/answer). Any of these slots may be filled by one or more sentences, but a sense of closure results only when the pattern has been completed, aided by semantic and structural cues along the way.

Students who are given exercises in tracing equivalence chains, lexical transitions, and grammatical links—the succession of content words and form words and their grammatical relations—all of which Becker explains in greater detail in his article, acquire an internalized sense of paragraph patterns that, in turn, gives them confidence in their own abilities to choose paragraphing without reference to set models.

In "A Generative Rhetoric of the Paragraph," Francis Christensen explains a different principle of paragraphing.[12] He defines the paragraph as a "sequence of structurally related sentences" and proceeds to define the relationship in terms of levels of generality. The topic sentence is nearly always first because it is the top sentence; that is, it represents the highest level of generality. Other sentences in the paragraph are either subordinate (at a lower level of generality) or coordinate (on the same level of generality). David Karrfalt,[13] among others, has pointed out that Christensen's scheme does not account for

[11] *The Sentence and the Paragraph*, pp. 34–36.
[12] *The Sentence and the Paragraph*, pp. 20–32.
[13] *The Sentence and the Paragraph*, pp. 71–76.

paragraphs in which sentences in a subordinate sequence sometimes move to a higher level of generality.

Those who are interested can study Christensen's principles and diagramming in detail, but what is significant here for our purposes is the suggestion in Christensen's work that most of our thinking as we write proceeds on the basis of generality and particularity, back and forth in such a way as to make clearer what the nature of our thinking is. Further, the alternation of general and particular in sentences within paragraphs and among paragraphs within an essay sets up a rhythmic pattern that becomes a basis for determining when we have completed the whole. Our sense of incompleteness in an essay is frequently due to a lack of balance between the generalizations and the particulars. The thought may be complete, but not the structure.

The significance of the work of Christensen, Becker, Rodgers, and numerous others who have responded to their ideas is that we are now able to view the paragraph as a far more flexible unit than we previously thought and that the patterning of the whole essay is akin to the same kind of ebb and flow or stimulus and response or commitment and fulfillment that we experience in the making of paragraphs.

In terms of all these concepts, form and structure become something that happens, as Shahn says, finding form in the material available. I am convinced that attempts to get students to be aware of structure as a process of developing patterns *as they write* is more natural and productive than trying to get them to structure an essay completely in advance. After students have created their own forms, they can then test them by means of the outline; the outline as a test of structure is useful.

At one school where I taught, strong emphasis was placed on the outline as a planning device. All instructors were required to use a specified outline form, the main subtopics of which were to be phrased so that they represented predicate nominatives of a thesis statement. In order to accomplish this feat, students consistently had to begin their thesis statements with a number: three characteristics of the French Gothic cathedral

[are] I, II, III; or two chief reasons for the Democratic victory in 1976 [were] I, II; or three reasons I chose to go to college [were] I, II, III. Further, in this program, students were supposed to write their outlines before they wrote their themes, and the theme was often judged by the extent it executed the plan. Obviously, most students did what any self-respecting student would do; they wrote their papers first and designed a corresponding outline when they were finished. Since that same university had a common final examination, after which the papers were exchange-graded, we all had the opportunity to see how students in other classes performed. The remarkable thing—and it is worthy of remark—is that all of the students seemed to write exactly alike. Every paper was conceived in terms of three this or four that—what Roger Sale rather amusingly calls "three piles" without much interrelatedness.[14] The structures all seemed the same. The themes produced were stereotypes. The only ones that varied were written by students who either refused to use the form or for some reason had not been taught to use it. Their papers were not necessarily less organized; their themes simply took other shapes. My experience in that program made clear to me that content and form can be separated. Or, to put it another way, form can be arbitrarily imposed, but to do so is to interfere with an organic process that allows writers to structure their material flexibly. In the final analysis, they need to learn more about linking the "inner parts" than designing the outer shape.

At the end of his bibliographical essay on "Structure and Form in Non-Fiction Prose" in *Teaching Composition*, Richard Larson writes:

> Instead of talking about "good organization" in the abstract, or advocating one plan of organization in preference to all others, the teacher should recognize the interconnections of form and content, and help students quietly in the subtle and personal task of choosing a form that suits well their ideas and emphases.[15]

---

[14]*On Writing* (New York: Random House, 1970), p. 81.
[15]Ed. Gary Tate (Fort Worth, Texas: Texas Christian University Press, 1976), p. 71.

One of the significant words in this sentence is "personal"—"the personal task of choosing a form." Form is the reins we hold over thoughts and feelings. It is personal. The job of teaching structure is not to prescribe it, but to help students realize how they can perceive and create the patterns of their own thoughts.

REPRESENTATIVE PROJECTS

The aim of most of these projects is to make students conscious of structure so that they will internalize concepts that become the intuitive source for shaping content.

1. In order to create awareness of structure—call it plan, organization, or system—have students report on patterns they observe in settings or events familiar to them. Even though buildings on campus appear to have been built without plan, do we find ways to group them: lower campus and upper campus, sciences and humanities, on campus and off campus? Or do we use a central focus for structuring: outside the quad, around the library, about 10 o'clock in relation to the fountain? What structures are apparent in particular TV shows, sports events, church services? View a movie strictly in terms of parts and the development of them. Look at paintings or photographs in terms of arrangement. Then read an essay with the same awareness of parts and arrangement. Consider some things that seem to be formless. Why do we ordinarily prefer shape to shapelessness? What is the importance of structure in writing?

2. Look at several short poems in terms of structure. What patterns emerge? For instance, Eberhart's "The Groundhog" may be said to fall into five parts: specific experience, reaction$_1$, reaction$_2$, reaction$_3$, conclusion. Have students translate a matrix of this kind into a prose essay.

3. Transcribe the lines of a short poem so that it reads as prose. Then disarrange the sentences, number them, and ditto the new version. Ask students to put them in an order that works. Which sentence makes the most appropriate beginning? Can the sentences move from the particular to the general as well as from the general to the particular? Is a beginning sentence chosen for dramatic effect? Which sentence is an appropriate close? Why? What principles dictate the arrangement of the sentences in between? Repetition? Structure words? Thematic connections? Reference words with antecedents in other sentences? Syntactic patterns?

If the exercise is carefully done, the rearrangement will involve almost every principle of structure: beginning, ending, orderly development in terms of grammatical and logical relations, coherence, and unity. After students compare their own versions with one another, they of course should see the original. They can then see clearly what the author's specific purpose may have been by choosing a particular arrangement.

Obviously, all poems will not serve this purpose. Workable examples include Elizabeth Bishop's "Filling Station," Wallace Stevens' "Disillusionment at Ten O'Clock," Kenneth Rexroth's "Spring," Edwin Arlington Robinson's "Bewick Finzer," and Robinson Jeffers' "The Bloody Sire" or "The Coast-Road."

4. Retype a short essay with all indentation removed. Number the sentences for convenience. Ask students to indicate where they would paragraph and for what reasons. Discuss the variations. Note particularly the points of strongest agreement. Finally, look at the original. What commentary does the exercise make upon the nature of paragraphing?

5. Examine the opening paragraphs of six or seven essays in an anthology to see what commitment the openings imply about the development of the essay. By their phrasing, do the writers indicate that they will enumerate evidence, compare, illustrate, treat causes, or proceed in some other way? The test of the structure is then the degree to which the commitment is fulfilled.

10

Teaching Words and Their Use

To many teachers, the word as a linguistic unit seems to be the beginning and end of writing. Perhaps. More often, I think, the fleeting thought, the vague notion, the undefined impulse is the beginning of writing. Or a motive. The word is the formulation of the idea or feeling. The exact word, the most appropriate word, the most challenging word may well be the end of the process; that is, reconsidering words during the revision stage can be the ultimate refinement of what we have written. To be unduly concerned about exactness in the middle of a thought may cause us to lose the thought altogether.

As writers, our concerns with the word vary. The important thing at the start is to get thoughts verbalized. At a later stage, the words can be reconsidered, rearranged, or simply rejected because they are unnecessary. The teaching of diction, therefore, can take several different focuses: utilitarian, rhetorical, and aesthetic. These cannot be totally separated, but the needs of students will determine where the chief emphasis will lie.

The first and most essential consideration of a utilitarian nature is the extent of an individual's vocabulary. It is axiomatic that we have at least three different vocabularies—our recognition vocabulary, our writing vocabulary, and our speaking vocabulary, each in that order with a decreasing number of words. The issue in the classroom is not to get more people to talk like books, but to get students to transfer more of their recognition/ reading vocabulary into writing. A teacher will succeed in getting students to do this only if students know that they are not going to get clobbered for trying and perhaps failing.

Teaching vocabulary at the high school and college levels remains an enigma. We all recognize that we learn words most readily in context, usually through reading, and absorb their meanings by repetition. Yet the question remains whether exercises in vocabulary building are of any use whatsoever. Lists are useful only to the extent that they acquaint students with some words that their limited reading experience has not provided them. Of far greater value are dictionary exercises that play upon the fascination that history holds for many people. Finding out that *gubernatorial*—a word that gets some prominence at least every four years—derives from a Latin root meaning "the helmsman of a boat" suggests to most people almost immediately the cliché that is equally common in election years: the ship of state. The kinds of exercises that are included in handbooks and rhetorics also explore variations of connotation among words that dictionaries and thesauruses suggest are coordinate and interchangeable. In these matters, vocabulary building and word-awareness can be combined with a study of the history of the language—how words are borrowed, how they are derived, how their meanings and values change.

But I must admit that studying vocabulary by studying the development of the language is a sophisticated technique for students who no longer make the most basic errors, and perhaps never did. I refer to the kinds of errors by students of basic writing that Mina Shaughnessy describes in Chapter 6 of *Errors and Expectations*.[1] Among these is the unidiomatic use of prepositions and other particles following nouns, verbs, and adjec-

---

[1] (New York: Oxford University Press, 1977).

tives. Our response to errors of this kind is first one of dissonance; we know something is wrong, although we may not be
able to explain more than to say that "to identify to" is unidiomatic. Idiom, of course, is intuitive, and we distinguish such
usages not on the basis of logic, but on the basis of our accumulated experience with words. Given relatively unfamiliar words,
even the sophisticated writer is likely to consult the dictionary
to see if it says anything about idiomatic uses following the
word.

A second category of error that Mina Shaughnessy notes is
the misuse of derivational suffixes in the formation of words.
For instance, a student invents a word like *preparance* presum-
ably on the basis of analogy with nouns like *inheritance* or *con-
veyance* or *utterance*. Of course, the formation of words by
means of suffixes is by no means systematic, but we can gain
familiarity with common forms by approaching words systemat-
ically. I refer to the kind of chart I first encountered in Frank
Flowers, *Practical Linguistics for Composition*,[2] a book no
longer in print. Flowers uses eight categories in his diagram. I
give here a somewhat simplified version. For those who are skit-
tish about grammatical terminology, the parts of speech can be
omitted from the chart.

Action	Agent Instrument	Act-Result	Description	Manner
[finite verb]	[noun]	[gerund or noun]	[adjective]	[adverb]
prepare	preparer	preparing preparation	prepared preparatory	preparedly preparatorily
quiz	quizzer	quiz quizzing	quizzical	quizzically

The technique is to give students only one of the forms
and ask them to generate the others, if that is possible. The

---

[2] (New York: Odyssey Press, 1968).

familiar word may lead to a less familiar but useful word: *micro-scope* to *microscopy*, for instance. The diagram can sometimes be completed, sometimes not, indicating where we lack words in the language and why coinages arise "to fill in the blanks."

At the top of the dittoed form I use for this purpose, I list all of the common verb, noun, adjective, and adverb suffixes. Apart from the list of noun suffixes, there are not many suffixes in the other categories, an instructive lesson in itself about the limitations of the language. If students, particularly in basic courses, work on five words per day using their dictionaries and then discuss their findings, I think gradually they will begin to think of new words they can use by extending the ones they already know.

What the diagram also invites is a discussion of forms that may exist in the dictionary but are seldom used. *Preparedly*, I should think, is rarely used. The noun form *preparer* is not listed in some collegiate dictionaries. That fact could be noted, as well as the substitute phrase we are more inclined to use: *one who prepares*. The lack of a word in the language often invites phrase structure. Some words at first only appear not to have a particular form. Given the verb *go*, most students will fail to fill in *goer* as an Agent. Yet when they are reminded that we commonly use it as a suffix, as in *theater-goer* or *opera-goer*, they see its place. Further, they observe how colloquial language tries to fill in the blanks where standard English seems to provide no word: *gone* is used as a descriptive term in *she is far gone*, and *liver* is used as a colloquial term for Agent in *he is a high liver*. *Lifer* is also a specialized term for "one serving a life sentence"—a slightly different context, but a related word.

In other instances, the diagram can be used to teach spelling changes, such as the shift from *maintain* to *maintenance* or *love* to *loving* to *lovable* (or *loveable*) or *lonely* to *loneliness*. On a particular day, one might provide five words that change their spellings in the same way as they change function: verbs like *bury, marry, empty, carry*, and *fly*, for instance. Repeated practice with this diagram will help students recognize some of the standard principles of spelling change, such as, in the list of verbs given, the change of *y* to *i* in words ending in *y* preceded by a consonant or doubling the consonant in monosyllables (like *quiz* in the diagram) when the monosyllable ends in a single consonant preceded by a vowel and the suffix begins with a vowel. *Plan, rob, sin, run,* and *swim* might be added to the list.

As a one-time exercise, the diagram has little value. It has to be used repeatedly, for then it can serve as a heuristic. The diagram helps to generate words by building on words we already know, and it helps to discover problem areas, whether those concern derivational suffixes, spelling changes, or substitute words for forms that do not exist. As an exercise, the diagram serves as a computer-like device for students to invent words and then test them against the dictionary. In time, it will become an internalized paradigm to be used as a point of reference. I was reminded of it recently when I read in program notes at the opera that "Don Giovanni was a notorious womanizer." My mind went from *woman* to *womanize* and back to *womanizer*—a terrible word, I thought. Indeed, it is a shorter expression than "a man who pursues women insatiably for sexual pleasure" and is different from just "seducer," but it has the same jargonish quality that coinages such as *finalize, remediate,* and *languaging* have. Using the diagram therefore requires some care and judgment. Students need to ask themselves whether all the forms they are capable of generating are capable of being used and accepted.

In the study of diction, utilitarian considerations therefore include learning new words, learning to spell them correctly, learning their precise meanings and common connotations, particularly those of a pejorative nature, in order to avoid obvious misuse. Besides accuracy in the use of words, there are rhetorical considerations, undoubtedly best studied in terms of sentences students have already written. These can be excerpted, dittoed, and discussed. How does moving an adverb to a new position change the emphasis? How does a squinting modifier cause ambiguity or unintended humor? How does a combination of too many *s*'s create more sound than sense? How does the substitution of a more concrete word for an abstract one sharpen the meaning? How does the addition of modifiers particularize and strengthen the thought? How many words act only as dead-wood, not even serving as fillers to make the sentence rhythmically satisfying? What words clearly mix varieties of usage inappropriate to the purpose of the writing? These are only a selection of rhetorical tests beyond matters of basic sentence construction, which we will discuss in Chapter 12.

I have included usage among rhetorical considerations because it seems to me the only sensible way to deal with an otherwise difficult issue. Individual writers can make up their own minds and make their own choices about language depending upon the circumstances in which they find themselves. Of course, they have to be aware of choices to make, which choices make a difference, and to whom.[3] Students in school in most instances operate under conventional constraints, unless a teacher thinks that no one should attempt to change the language habits of anyone else—an attitude that seems to deny the function of the English teacher. Whether the English teacher makes a declaration of intention or not, that person is constantly influencing the language habits of students, if by no other way than creating a consciousness of and conscience about language. If this is not so, why do we encounter the ubiquitous phrase when we identify ourselves as English teachers: "Well, I suppose I'll have to watch my grammar"?

It is one thing to point out that usage is a matter of individual choice; it is another to weigh the practical situation. Supporters of *The Students' Right to Their Own Language,* for instance, point out that a viable alternative doesn't exist.[4] Society clearly discriminates against those whose language does not conform reasonably well to standard norms—norms that are taught and perpetuated by the schools, although one should question whether these are not perpetuated more by society in

[3]Robert M. Gorrell, "Usage as Rhetoric," *College Composition and Communication,* 28 (1977), 20-25.

[4]Special issue, *College Composition and Communication,* 25 (Fall, 1974). Available from the National Council of Teachers of English.

general than by the schools in particular. Learning the prestige dialect, essentially "white man's English," many language experts would say, is a forced choice.

My purpose here is not to argue a highly complicated question, but simply to point out that it is one thing to make usage a rhetorical issue (some might say "academic") and another to make it a moral issue. A teacher can be flexible, which is not the same as condoning anything. But a teacher can recognize that all dialects can at times be effective and valuable; that the use of one dialect or another is not a sign of intelligence or superior language ability; that a teacher's expectations often depend upon whether a student is speaking or writing; that usage is closely related to what the writer or speaker hopes to accomplish; that we can all try to pare our prejudices and pet peeves about language; that though some people will argue that standard English is only a myth, it is a hard, undeniable reality to those who do not have access to it; that prescriptive usage satisfies those who are constantly seeking authority in language because rules relieve them of the responsibility of making choices; that as teachers we need to think through the implications of our own position. What expectations are we setting? What values are we perpetuating? What is our function in the school and in society? What is our responsibility to the individual student? Usage is more than a few prescriptions about polite use of language. More often than we would care to admit, it is the shibboleth that opens or closes a door to someone who wants to enter.

Aesthetic considerations in the teaching of words are more difficult to define because they depend to such a great extent upon an individual's attitude toward language. Many students think of language only as a tool of communication. They fail to realize that we create an image of ourselves by the way we use language. We are not just shapers of language; language shapes us as well.

A number of years ago, a senior professor in my department, who at that time was teaching his regular assignment of freshman composition, made an observation I have always remembered, mainly because he called my attention to the importance of one's basic attitude toward language. He was telling me about several foreign students he had in his classes and observed that all of them were doing a better job than the native-born students. Then he gave his reason: "I think they are all doing better because each of them has a respect for language that our students don't have." I have come to like the phrase—"a respect for language"—because it incorporates that same sense of awe that we express when we say we respect electricity or we respect a storm. These, like language, are vast unharnassed resources that only with knowledge and care we learn to control. Great numbers of our students, including those who are preparing to teach in secondary schools, and even doctoral students in English who will be professors of the discipline, think they have no obligation whatsoever to study the language. Study of the structure and development of the English language characteristically has to be required in English departments. No wonder that often those who have learned to respect the language have come to that realization through their own creative efforts. They know the power of the use and abuse of language.

I realize that I have sermonized a bit in the preceding paragraph, but as teachers we should realize that our attitudes toward language will affect the attitudes of our students. I remember one teacher who began every class session in freshman composition by reading a poem—no commentary, no discussion, no questions, just the reading. To him, the poem simply embodied language at its best. That was his way of saying language deserves respect.

If "respect for language" as a phrase conjures up notions that are too dour, there is another equally important consideration, again all too often neglected in the schools. Call it playfulness with language—taking delight in the word itself. I remember recently having the word *Havasupai* pop into my mind one morning in a completely unexpected way, especially since as I later learned I must have last encountered the word almost twenty years before. The word haunted me for days until I found out in the library—not without considerable effort—that the Havasupai are a tribe of Indians living in the Grand Canyon in Arizona. I remembered the word, not because I have any special interest in Indian history or Indian lore, but because it is a word I like to say and, when I am reminded of it, one that sticks in my mind like a catchy tune. I have fun with it.

What does that personal digression have to do with writing? To be sure, it has nothing to do with anyone else's writing, but it has much to do with my own intuitive sense of word choice and my particular delight in the sound of words. I like to read Gertrude Stein whether she makes sense or not.

Many students don't learn what their capacities for language are until they are encouraged to experiment with it. They can begin by observing—collecting bumper stickers, puns in advertisements, coinages and compounds. Then they can try some of their own. Some of them even discover a remarkable capacity they didn't know they had. But, more importantly, they all begin to see that language is not all seriousness. They can enjoy words for sounds and magic, as children almost always do. Of course, grown-ups also don't do much skipping, but they miss a lot because they gave up the practice a long time ago.[5]

REPRESENTATIVE PROJECTS

1. Have students focus on the printed advertising of one product: liquor, automobiles, cosmetics, or a particular item of clothing. Examine the language used in terms of (1) the connotations of the brand name, (2) emotional and logical appeals (sex, status, economy, efficiency), (3) the categories of words used (technical, slang, conversational), (4) puns, metaphors, and euphemisms, (5) deliberate distortions, misspellings, invented spellings, and ungrammatical forms. Have the students compare the effects of various advertisements.

2. Have students listen to a comedian or read a humorous writer whose humor depends mainly upon malapropisms,

---

[5]For innumerable suggestions, see Peter Farb, *Word Play* (New York: Bantam Books, 1975), and Don and Alleen Nilsen, *Language Play: An Introduction to Linguistics* (Rowley, Mass.: Newbury House Publishers, 1978).

puns, or mispronunciations. Have them record examples and examine the source of the humor.

3. Have students look in the daily newspaper for evidence of language that stereotypes. What adjectives and verbs are used when a news report concerns a woman of high social standing, an outstanding sports figure, an unpopular foreign official, a teenage criminal, the local mayor? Have students try to categorize the stereotypes and list the words that create that particular image. Is there evidence of sexism, racism, or prejudice?

4. Have students collect the wording of twenty or twenty-five bumper stickers. What devices of language are used? Have them look for puns, ambiguities, allusions, rhymes, repetitions, and any other devices that make them memorable.

5. Have students create their own Book of Lists:
   a. Their ten favorite words (the ones they use on every occasion possible)
   b. Ten technical terms they are familiar with (spelled correctly)
   c. Ten slang words or phrases they commonly use
   d. Ten foreign phrases they can use accurately in English contexts
   e. Ten obvious clichés they recognize
   f. Ten recent words they have learned
   g. Ten words they recognize, but are constantly uncertain of their meanings
   h. Ten words they would use in writing but never speak
   i. Ten acronyms they can explain
   j. Ten words that use reduplication (shilly shally, riff-raff, hustle bustle)
   k. Ten words derived from place names
   Have students add other lists that interest them.

6. Reproduce a prose passage with certain key adjectives and verbs deleted. Indicate the omissions by a blank. Have

students use structural and contextual clues to choose a word that will substitute. Compare various suggestions; compare with the original. The exercise tests word sense and the ability to use clues to fill in the blanks. It also identifies clichés. If half of the class uses the same word, very likely that choice is hackneyed.

11

Teaching Mechanics

We sometimes overlook the fact that mechanics is the one element of composing that is exclusively graphic. Juncture is of course a part of all speaking, but at such breaks we do not need to decide between a period or semicolon or comma. We merely pause. Both capitalization and spelling are also graphic. If something is typed or printed, then typography becomes a part of mechanics as well. In this chapter, however, we will be concerned only with punctuation, capitalization, and spelling.

Almost inevitably by the advanced high school years and certainly in the college years, teachers have adopted an aloof attitude toward mechanics. The errors are there, but teachers rationalize that they must concern themselves with the more important matters of substance and structure. The irony is that a similar rationalization has gone on throughout the school years, so that the students' exposure to systematic instruction in mechanics has been rare and, at best, sporadic. Teachers who insist on correctness unfortunately gain reputations as pedants and sticklers.

Yet, at the same time, each one of the gainsayers of correctness reads what is printed and assumes it will be completely accurate. In fact, most readers are not even aware of the assumption they make, because errorless writing and printing do not cause dissonance. Usually, they fail to think about graphics because mechanics seem to be neutral. I want to emphasize "seem to be neutral," because I would argue that punctuation is not neutral and can be regarded as an element of style just as characteristic words and structures are.

We should also note that the tolerance of mechanical errors that we find among many English teachers, despite their traditional image as purists, is not shared by the general public. The public definition of "basics" includes legible handwriting, correct spelling, accurate punctuation, and what is usually called "good grammar," a phrase used to cover standard usage. It is conceivable that a definition of basics concocted by English teachers would include these only in deference to public demand.

Thus, to start with, we have a problem about attitudes—the attitude of students, the attitude of teachers, and the attitude of the public, which may include a good number of parents who want their children to get instruction in "basics" that they did not get. Teachers need to think of the differences in attitude that exist in a particular classroom at a particular time, especially about their own attitude in relation to that of the students and their parents. How do we avoid an antagonistic position? And how do we avoid undermining an accepted—call it even an old-fashioned—value of correctness?

My own position may already be clear. I want my students to be confident about the use of mechanics, not because I think correctness, like cleanliness, is next to godliness, but because I think mechanics should in no way be an obstacle to thought; that is, a writer should not have to worry about mechanics any more than a good typist ought to be concerned about which fingers to use. Furthermore, only with assurance about essential uses of punctuation and capitalization can one begin to talk about the more sophisticated and flexible uses of mechanics for rhetorical purposes. Or, in terms we used earlier, mastery of the productive skills makes possible inventive uses. Writers cannot get a feeling of flexibility with language until they have learned to master the basic tools and overcome doubts about how to use them.

Let's talk first about learning the basic uses of punctuation. The problem is not too difficult to analyze. Most handbooks give a clue: nine to thirteen uses of the comma, two to five uses of the semicolon, four to five uses of the colon, one to seven uses of the dash, exclusive of guidelines for the use of periods, question marks, exclamation points, parentheses, brackets, quotation marks, ellipsis points, hyphens, apostrophes, and slashes. Punctuation seems to be based on an endless list of rules, too long to remember and too confusing to apply. Thus, many students turn to the pause method—that is, putting in some mark of punctuation whenever they pause—but of course they do not mark *all* pauses, and what they do they do with inconsistency. They usually end up with more punctuation than necessary, tending to clutter the prose rather than clarify it.

Even some writers who punctuate with reasonable accuracy and consistency claim not to know what they are doing. What they mean is that they can't recite the rules. They depend to a great extent upon sensitivity to structures and their intuitive sense of juncture and closure. Whether or not they can label an introductory adverbial clause is not as important as the fact that they recognize the structural unit and separate it from what follows with a comma. Less confident writers are likely to confuse their strong sense of closure at major junctures with grammatical completeness. Thus, they tend to punctuate the end of a dependent clause with a period as if it were an independent clause. Unless the intuitive sense of closure is counterbalanced by syntactic certainty, all kinds of blunders can occur. We have to face the fact that about 75 percent of punctuation is structurally based. The remainder is conventional, like dates, omissions, quotations, abbreviations, and so on.

There is no question that grammatical knowledge can help with punctuation. Some errors that at first appear to be structural errors are errors in punctuation. A relative clause may be punctuated as a sentence simply because the student doesn't know what it is and doesn't recognize that it belongs to the previous sentence and should be attached to it with a comma. Further, grammatical knowledge can help in the development of prose style if it is used to show how punctuation works in conjunction with principles of embedding and branching. The study of sentence construction should also be a study of punctuation.

But the rules remain, and they seem fragmentary and arbitrary. Few students are ever subjected to a systematic approach, probably because too few teachers are themselves aware of a systematic approach. There is not one system—one description. Like systems of grammar, there may be several. Individuals can even work out their own. Let me give two illustrations.

In *Errors and Expectations*, Mina Shaughnessy points out that inexperienced writers are limited mainly to the use of periods and commas, with some uncertainty even about their use.[1] If we begin with the assumption that the period and the comma are the basic marks of punctuation (they do almost everything punctuation needs to do) and all of the other marks are sophisticated variations of those two, then we have the basis for developing a system for those writers. If we define the period as a terminal mark (a stopping and separating function), then it is easy to see how the question mark and the exclamation point are variations of it. In fact, the question mark is so completely unnecessary in the language that we usually find ourselves using a period instead. Questions, except for intonation questions, are signalled structurally. A phrase like "do you know" indicates that a question is coming. In "Poetry and Grammar," Gertrude Stein says it might be all right to use a question mark as a brand on cattle, but as a mark of punctuation it is completely uninteresting: "A question is a question, anybody can know that a question is a question and so why add to it the question mark when

---

[1] (New York: Oxford University Press, 1977), p. 17.

it is already there when the question is already there in the writing."[2] She puts exclamation points and quotation marks in the same category.

If we define the comma, the second basic mark, as an interrupting mark (a break, but going on), we can point out that semicolons and colons can substitute for the combining function of commas; dashes, parentheses, and brackets can substitute for the enclosing function; and colons and dashes can substitute for the introducing function. These are basic uses of punctuation. This is as much "system" as anyone needs for a start. There is no point in concentrating on the exceptions until

To terminate and separate	To combine and separate*	To introduce	To enclose
period			
exclamation point			
question mark			
	comma	comma	commas
	semicolon		
	colon	colon	
	dash	dash	dashes
			parentheses
			brackets
			quotation marks
	hyphen (compounds)		

* Some text writers try to distinguish between a combining function and a separating function. The distinction is a fine one. I have chosen to interpret certain uses of the comma and semicolon as both combining and separating. The writer may choose to combine two sentences because they are closely related, but separates them with a semicolon to mark the juncture. A writer less concerned about the combining function would use a period.

---

[2] In *Modern Essays on Writing and Style*, ed. Paul C. Wermuth (2nd ed., New York: Holt, Rinehart and Winston, 1969), p. 73.

students have a firm grasp of the primary uses. Once they know these, all the rest is illustration, practice, and application.

Students who characteristically use the full range of punctuation but use it erratically can profit from viewing the system diagrammatically. Instead of beginning only with the period and comma and extending to the other marks of punctuation, this second approach shows the marks all at once in relation to one another (see the diagram, opposite page).

In order to simplify the diagram, I have not included the function of indicating omission, marked sometimes by the period (for abbreviations), the comma (the omitted verb in parallel constructions), the dash (incomplete utterance), ellipsis points (omitted words in quotations), the hyphen (omitted prefix or suffix), and the apostrophe (contractions). These are all specialized and conventional uses and need not confuse this diagram.

I have already commented on the limited uses of the question mark and exclamation mark as occasional substitutes for the period. Note further the implications of the diagram. Of the five marks listed under "To combine and separate," the hyphen combines words to form compounds; the comma, colon, dash (and sometimes the semicolon as a substitute for the comma) combine parts of sentences (series of words, phrases, and clauses, for instance); and the comma, semicolon, and, occasionally, the colon and dash combine main clauses. The differences, of course, have to be explained. The comma is used when the connective between two sentences is a coordinating conjunction; the semicolon, when the connective is a conjunctive adverb or when it is omitted altogether; the colon, when the two clauses are phrased so that the first clause sets up an expectation to be met in the second; and the dash as a loose and indiscriminate substitute for all of these.

These are only a sampling of the kinds of comparisons and connections that can be made from the chart. Once the basic uses are clarified, the chart can be used to illustrate what flexibilities exist in the use of punctuation for rhetorical purposes. Dashes as enclosing marks do interrupt more strongly than commas. Parentheses accommodate asides, although the choice of dashes or parentheses might be a personal preference. The colon in nineteenth-century prose was used virtually as a substitute for the semicolon. It can still be used to set up a special kind of anticipation between the combined parts. Once students become familiar with the uses and the allowable flexibilities, they begin to show their preferences. Clearly the period and the comma are utility marks, generally used and basically neutral in their effect. But in time some students become dash-people, some colon freaks, and some even semicolon lovers. All of us actually show a preference for particular marks of punctuation just as we show a preference for particular structures. We can keep the prose tight and controlled by preferring periods, commas, and semicolons to dashes, parentheses, and colons. We can loosen the prose, make it more casual, by preferring those marks that have fewer constraints on their use. The dash can be as flexibly used as the comma, but its uses are less precisely defined. It therefore substitutes for almost any of the other marks. It is the mark of free association. It is sometimes the mark of desperation.

Once we get across the idea that punctuation is functional, not only that it promotes readability, but that it also gives us stylistic freedom to arrange and rearrange words, we should be able to get away from the notion of punctuation-as-additive, something that can be added perhaps by someone else after the job of writing is done. Punctuating ought to be an integral part of the process.

Capitalization, one must admit, is less integral to the process, although capitalization at the beginning of a sentence has a structural basis. It might seem to most teachers that capitalization is not a problem. For most students, it may cause no more doubts than it does to most of us when we have to decide whether to write "go west" or "go West." But for many others, capitalization is apparently no more systematic than punctuation.

For the past seven or eight years, I have read writing samples written by students applying for special admission to the University of Washington under EOP. These are mainly minority students. Two tendencies can be noted among different groups. The first is what appears to be cultivated eccentricity— no capitalization whatsoever, even at the beginning of sentences or of the pronoun *I*, although most of these same students will not defy God. The other tendency is to write a kind of Germanic style, capitalizing nouns with abandon. I must confess that I have not investigated the reason for the second mannerism, although it seems to have a rhetorical basis. Words that are capitalized are important words the writer wants to call attention to.

Among the numerous writing ailments that plague students, capitalization seems to be a minor one—a rash that can be eliminated easily or possibly even outgrown. One of the reasons is that the rules are relatively simple and clearcut. The crux is to learn the rules.

Misspelling, however, is another issue altogether, one so deeply rooted in the psyche that those who chronically misspell have built up defenses that no teacher is likely to penetrate. I must confess that in thirty years of teaching I have never known an adult who overcame the problem of very bad spelling. That is not to say there are none. I simply have not met one. My experience may be reason to despair and to give up entirely on adults who are bad spellers. I think not, however.

Apart from the very bad spellers whose problems may spring from neurological dysfunctions, almost anyone can become a better speller. There are a few facts that as teachers we overlook, some of them in the category of the self-evident:

1. Almost everyone spells more words correctly than incorrectly.
2. Those that are misspelled can usually be categorized; that is, we misspell words in characteristic ways. This provides the hope for cure.
3. Good spellers are not good at faking misspelling. If they try to imitate a bad speller, they make too many different kinds

of errors. Bad spellers usually misspell in one or two categories. Awareness of patterns helps to eliminate many of the
individual misspellings.

4. More misspellings occur inside a word (medially) than at the
   beginning or end.

5. One of the commonest misspellings is mistaking the vowel in
   an unaccented syllable because all vowels in this position are
   usually pronounced with a neutral sound, ordinarily referred
   to as the schwa (ə).

6. Since the patterns of misspelling are individual, diagnosis
   needs to be made on an individual basis; the only spelling
   demons are the ones that threaten us individually.

7. It is more satisfying to be a good speller than a bad speller;
   every bad speller has to believe that learning to spell better
   has positive benefits that are worth the effort to learn.

8. The typewriter is one of the overlooked devices for teaching
   spelling. It provides a different view of the word.

9. Learning to spell is a continuing process because we constantly encounter new words. Accurate spelling requires a
   keen eye.

10. Millions of people have mastered the English spelling sys-
    tem. It is not beyond the abilities of most educable people.

Even though many writers do not want to be concerned
with punctuation, capitalization, and spelling, they have to be
because the reader cannot easily do without them. All of the
mechanics are signals of one kind or another. Sending out the
wrong signals is misdirecting the reader or, more often, momen-
tarily delaying the decoding process. Readers don't like obstacles. Even though mechanics are certainly not the most important thing in the world of writing, they are certainly obvious
when they are misused. And when they are misused, they create
an impression of illiteracy more readily than almost any other
element of writing. The public at large seems not to regard
diction, structure, and style to the extent that it regards mechanics, possibly because the accurate use of mechanics seems the
most elementary. If punctuation, capitalization, and spelling are
learned early so that they can be used intuitively but soundly in
the same way that we write sentences, attention to them, then,

should not divert us as writers from more essential matters or distract those who are readers.

REPRESENTATIVE PROJECTS

1. The proofreading test remains one of the best ways to talk about the use of mechanics in context. Reproduce a published passage with all punctuation and capitalization removed. Misspell a few words, but don't load sentences with too many errors. Ask students to proofread. Then have them compare versions, give reasons for using particular marks, and finally refer to the original. Stress that the original is the author's version. Other interpretations are possible.

2. Thinking again of punctuation as interpretation, examine an essay in terms of what related but different punctuation would do to the meaning or tone. Would commas work as well as dashes? Would a period create a significantly different effect from a semicolon? To what degree is the writer's punctuation conventional or idiosyncratic?

3. Have students examine a passage of nineteenth-century prose. To what extent does the punctuation vary from contemporary standards?

4. Students are not likely to gain confidence with punctuation unless they know the difference between restrictive and nonrestrictive: restrictive appositives as opposed to nonrestrictive ones, nonrestrictive phrases and clauses as opposed to restrictive ones. The principle needs to be established, and it can certainly be best explained if students have some basic knowledge of grammar. Have students examine each other's papers for structures that are restrictive or nonrestrictive. Then, of course, see if they are punctuated correctly or whether punctuation is unnecessarily used.

5. Over a period of time, accumulate examples from student writing that appear to be structural errors (failure to write a complete sentence) but are actually errors in punctuation. A fragment may actually be a phrase that belongs to the previous sentence and should be attached to it with a comma, but the writer does not know how to manipulate the punctuation. Or run-on sentences may be seen not as a failure to write complete sentences, but a failure to punctuate them correctly. If students are asked merely to alter punctuation, not to change the wording, they may possibly see the source of their errors.

12

Teaching Style

Anyone who has taught composition for any length of time knows that eventually, usually one day right after class, a student will ask, "What can I do to improve my style?" It is a question of such inevitableness that a beginning teacher of composition ought to have some kind of answer ready.

My own goes something like this: I don't think there is anything I can do directly to help you improve your style. I can help you with some of your sentences, with the choice of words, with the organization of ideas, and a number of other things. Then you can see whether you think your style has improved. But I don't know how to work on style as a thing by itself. If the student takes this reply as a sign of my incompetence and presses the matter further, I can give a theoretical basis for my answer.

Every teacher of composition ought to have some kind of working definition of style. By "working definition" I mean one that gives both teacher and student a handle on the term. There are innumerable essays *on* style, but reading them does not necessarily make students more skillful in creating stylistic effects, that is, in making the choices that will affect style. My response to students who want to know what they can do to improve is based on a concept of style as an aggregate of the lexical and structural features of a particular work. More simply put, the words and arrangements in a particular context produce an effect that we can label style. We don't put style into something or add it on. We produce it by the things we do. It emerges. Style results from choices we make.

With this working definition, it is only fair to add a few explanations:

1. Choice affects style, but every choice is not equally significant. Some choices tend to be neutral. The substitution of *but* for *however* may be considerably less significant stylistically than the change of *man* to *person.*

2. In terms of style as an aggregate, there is no such thing as stylelessness. Yet some styles are so completely neutral and uninteresting that the resulting writing can be characterized as having no style; such styles have no distinctiveness or identity.

3. Identity of style is based on individual choices. Identity does not mean eccentricity, but it does imply characteristic choices and combinations by an individual that deviate from the most predictable norm. The most normative style is the Plain Style, often called the encyclopedic style, because it tends to neutralize the individual voice. For this reason, it is used for utilitarian kinds of prose that all writers ought to be able to write as the situation demands. The minutes of a meeting need only be factual. When facts are of first importance, as they often are in reports, digests, and contracts, the Plain Style is appropriate. As soon as a note of appeal or persuasion enters, the element of voice then has an effect. The Plain Style is a good style for the purposes it best serves.

In terms of the definition of style as a composite effect, it should be apparent that as teachers we treat elements of style in almost everything we do from the first day in the composition class. There are ways of determining the statistical dimensions of a writer's style by counting the length of the sentences, the

proportion of short words to long ones, the degree of subordination and coordination—and the list can go on[1]—but after we
have done those things we have not fully accounted for the total
impressions we get from the prose. At times, it is necessary to
confront specifically the three main elements that affect style:
the self, the audience, and the strategies we employ in writing.

When I once asked a group of students to write down what
they thought they needed to know to become better writers,
one student wrote: "I've never yet found out how much of myself I should put into papers of different types." Clearly what
was puzzling this student was the relation of the self to style.
Students who in high school or college are forbidden to use the
first-person pronoun in anything they write are confused, because they know they are writing about their own experiences
and their own opinions. How does a teacher demonstrate how
the self affects style, even if the first-person pronoun is not
there?

One particularly useful method is to introduce Wayne
Booth's concept of the rhetorical stance, referred to in Chapter
5. I repeat the definition here. He defines it as "a stance which
depends on discovering and maintaining in any writing situation
a proper balance among three elements that are at work in any
communicative effort: the available arguments about the subject
itself, the interests and peculiarities of the audience, and the
voice, the implied character of the speaker."[2] He refers to three
corruptions of this stance: the pedant's stance that depends solely on the arguments and forgets the audience; the advertiser's
stance that plays on audience response and forgets substance;
and the entertainer's stance that depends solely on the personality of the writer or speaker. These can be defined and developed
in different ways. The important thing is that by this means
students have a way of talking about style, perhaps the styles of

---

[1] See Appendix A, "Styles and Statistics," in Walker Gibson, *Tough, Sweet &
Stuffy* (Bloomington: Indiana University Press, 1966), pp. 113-140.
[2] "The Rhetorical Stance," *College Composition and Communications,* 14
(1963), 141.

a lecturer on campus, a TV commentator, a politician, an essayist, and, above all, themselves as they respond to each other's writing. Trying to determine the rhetorical stance of a piece of prose becomes a basic exercise in recognizing the means of persuasion originally defined by Aristotle: by reason (*logos*), by emotion (*pathos*), and by the implied character of the speaker (*ethos*).

Recently I came upon a headline in the newspaper that read: "Class helps students 'find' their movement." The article featured a dance class at one of the local community colleges. The phrasing of the headline, based on a statement by the teacher, impressed me as a novel way of describing dance instruction, but then it occurred to me that every writing class ought to do something similar: it ought to help students "find" their own style, that most characteristic way of their own expression. All too often, I fear, we are more interested in imposing a standard style—the Plain Style—upon them. It is simpler to evaluate. Yet becoming aware of "voices"—the personae of prose writers—fascinates beginning students of writing, many of whom still cling to the notion that writing should not show personal traces.

Anyone who has not previously taught composition may consider the matter of voice somewhat esoteric, the kind of interest a graduate student might have in Jane Austen, but not high school or college freshmen in their own prose. The truth is that students find the emphasis on voice fascinating as long as the instructor keeps the discussion nontheoretical and works with their own writing or with selections by established writers.

It is difficult to separate topics like voice, involvement, subjectivity, tone, and point of view because they all overlap. And there is no reason to try to parcel them out. Characterizing a voice or defining the persona that they as readers perceive is a way of dispelling the elusiveness of style, for the students are actually picking up the clues in the prose—elements of that final composite—that permit them to say that something is ironic, humorous, understated or exaggerated, restrained or flamboyant, formal or casual. Students will also begin to realize that the idea of the one true self is basically a fallacy. We may eventually develop a marked style of our own, but we will always assume various voices depending upon the purpose and occasion. What we can often note among beginning writers is the tendency to mix voices—to shift abruptly, as Walker Gibson observes, from the podium to the locker room.[3] The issue is not that formal is good and casual bad, but that the two—and the strategies that create one effect or the other—are inconsistent with one another. The reader is jolted.

What kinds of voices do students themselves find unpleasant? Let them begin with speaking voices. Those that are too loud? Too sharp? Too syrupy? They will of course have their own terms. What voices are ineffectual? Why? Most of the responses will be made in terms of an individual's sense of the normative—the intuitive center of balance we have already spoken of in Chapter 4. The unpleasant and ineffectual will exceed their normal range of tolerance.

It is not a far jump from talking about the speaking voice to talking about the voice in prose that we perceive rather than hear. What strategies of language throw readers off balance by violating their expectations? Obscenities? Illiteracies? Ornateness? Obscurity? Buffoonery? What these considerations open up is the regard writers must have for readers if they want to be read voluntarily. The significant difference between classroom writing and almost all other writing is that the teacher is essentially a captive reader, although I have known a few teachers who will draw a line across a paper after several paragraphs and say that they refuse to read further until so-and-so—whatever represents the major offense—has been eliminated. It's a gesture of righteous indignation. It also asserts that teachers have minimum standards that have to be met. These teachers do not let themselves be captives.

In the classroom, it is difficult to escape the hard fact that the teacher is usually the only reader. The teacher is therefore the audience, and the style will no doubt be accommodated to

[3] "The 'Speaking Voice' and the Teaching of Composition," text of a kinescope produced by the Commission on English of the College Entrance Examination Board.

the teacher. That's not all bad if the teacher is someone whom the student respects, feels comfortable with, and wants to write for. I have upon occasion simply said to students in my classes that they should write for me, not so much me in the role of a professor who is going to give a grade, but me in the role of reader/critic or editor, who is going to make a professional judgment about their writing.

To speak of the teacher or even students in the classroom as an audience is simple, but we have to recognize that the audience for whom we write is not usually so accessible. More often we have no clear sense of audience. How, then, can we talk about an audience factor if the audience is out there somewhere, completely unknown, maybe at the time of our writing even nonexistent? If writers are supposed to consider the audience, what are they supposed to think about when they begin to put pen to paper?

We must of course seriously ask ourselves if the self and the audience are separate or actually one and the same. In *A Rhetoric of Motives*, Kenneth Burke writes: "A man can be his own audience, insofar as he, even in his secret thoughts, cultivates certain ideas or images for the effect he hopes they may have upon him; he is here what Mead would call 'an "I" addressing its "me".' . . ."[4] This is the ideal audience—an audience of other I's, with the same preferences, tastes, and arguments as our own—a completely receptive and nonthreatening audience.

In the sense of the "I addressing its me," a writer is not writing for a vague collective audience, but creating an audience. Another way of saying the same thing is to think of the audience not so much as a group of people for whom one is writing as a set of values or a set of expectations one tries to meet. These values and expectations can be highly generalized. In fact, the more specific they become, the more inhibiting they become. In the final analysis, as Walter Ong reminds us, there are only individual readers, not a collective audience.[5] The read-

---

[4](New York: George Braziller, Inc., 1955), p. 38.
[5]"The Writer's Audience Is Always a Fiction," *Publications of the Modern Language Association*, 90 (1975), 11.

ers who read, those who after the first paragraph continue to read further, those who persist—they are our audience. They are individual readers who tune in to the wave length on which we are broadcasting.

In argumentative writing, the expectations need to be altered somewhat. We must assume that among individual readers there are those who hold views different from our own, despite the fact that, even on controversial questions, we tend to read the writers with whom we agree. But even if readers hold opposite views, we must assume that they are as reasonable as we consider ourselves. Otherwise, why write? No one writes to be disbelieved, even frauds. We seek acceptance for our views. Rhetorically, we make an appeal in two senses: we submit our case for acceptance, and we attempt to please. The audience determines the success or failure of that appeal.

Success or failure often depends upon the skill of the writer with words. Clearly, the limitation of beginning writers is their lack of a sense of strategy. The phrase almost immediately suggests an analogy with sports. Almost anyone can play a game, whatever it may be. The ones who excel are those who have a sense of strategy—those who know how the whole thing will develop and how individual movements and choices will affect the total outcome. I am talking, of course, about strategies of style. What are they?

In 1969, Winston Weathers and Otis Winchester published a text called *Copy and Compose: A Guide to Prose Style.*[6] It was a book based on a method of conscious imitation. In one section, the authors draw upon a vast catalogue of delightful-sounding tropes and schemes—epizeuxis, polysyndeton, symploce, and epanalepsis—illustrate them, and ask students to compose sentences in their own words using the devices. Unfortunately, the names that I take special delight in are major obstacles to most people, particularly those who think writing is a great mystery anyway, not realizing that if they have any sensi-

---

[6](Englewood Cliffs, N.J: Prentice-Hall.)

tivity to language at all they intuitively write many of these figures of speech without ever being aware that they have done so.

Imitation is a useful resource for making students aware of strategies of style, not imitation for the sake of copying but for the sake of discovery. When I use imitation as a teaching technique, I do not begin with a model I want students to imitate, but I have them choose a sentence that they have responded to in a special way in the course of their reading. Ordinarily, as we read, one sentence after another reads meaningfully but inauspiciously; then one clicks. Sometimes that sentence is important because it states all that had gone before at a high level of generality. It capsulates the thought. But often, if it is a sentence of major importance in the development of the thought, the writer has also given it a form that expresses it to maximum advantage. At the conclusion of one section of a long speech in Peter Shaffer's play *Equus*, Dysart says, "Passion, you see, can be destroyed by a doctor. It cannot be created." The climactic phrasing of that thought, as well as the thought itself, makes those two sentences in the play memorable.

If I choose to imitate those particular sentences, I have to ask myself what I can write that can assume the form of Dysart's remarks. First, I have to analyze the structure of the sentences: the asymmetrical balance, the contrast of the two verbs, both in passive voice, the subject in first position, the prepositional phrase dropped in the second sentence, the parenthetical "you see" in the first sentence acting as a rhythmical filler. With these notes and a bit of experimentation, I come up with this sentence: Excess, I think, can be condemned by a critic. It cannot be condoned.

In contrast to other sentences I wrote and discarded as I worked on this imitation, this final one pleased me. My version is blander than Shaffer's, but then it is a blander topic. Perhaps the relation between the terms is not exactly the same, but that is something to be learned in itself—the qualities and subtleties that an imitator simply cannot reproduce. I have no reason to think I will ever use my sentence in another context, but in doing it I accomplished something else. By imitating, I got an insight into the inner workings of Shaffer's sentences, why they come off with the striking effect that they do. Imitation is a way of getting inside another writer's strategy, not just looking at it from the outside. And that should make me more aware of strategy.

By trying an exact imitation, students discover why some sentences work and possibly why others don't. They become aware of alliteration, the use of conjunctions in a series (polysyndeton), the repetition of words at the beginning of a series of phrases or sentences (anaphora), and, especially, the words in the original that are not imitable because in context they have an imaginative force that is derived from what I. A. Richards calls the "interinanimation of the meaning of words."[7] That kind of stylistic effect is unique.

Imitation is not easy, chiefly because imitation reverses the natural process of composing. Normally, we begin with a thought and find a shape to suit it. In exact imitation, we begin with a set structure and try to find a thought to fit it. Often it is impossible, especially if we try to imitate more than one or two sentences. Longer passages can be written in the manner of another writer, but they can seldom follow the precise pattern of another writer for very long.

Exact imitation, however, is especially worthwhile as a way of studying strategies of style, as a way of learning what writers do to create effects, and as a way of becoming more aware of the subtleties of style. What beginning writers also learn is that the rhetorical strategies that have elaborate names are not inaccessible at all. They come to us quite naturally in composing once we become aware of them. Imitation is a way of informing intuition.

Studies of syntactic maturity that have been made, especially those of Kellogg Hunt, indicate that mature writers, if

---

[7] *The Philosophy of Rhetoric* (New York: Oxford University Press, 1936), p. 69.

they wish to, have the capacity to combine sentences as a stylistic option, and they have a variety of syntactic resources to draw upon.[8] Other works on sentence combining, now proliferating after the initial pioneering work by Mellon and O'Hare, suggest that the ability to manipulate syntactic structures, which some teachers would see as a justification for the study of grammar, is a way of working on style. It is a good way unless sentence combining degenerates into doing workbook exercises, with the familiar result that students go through the motions of completing the exercises without absorbing the principles. As usual, a student's own prose is the best starting point. Combining as many sentences as possible is not necessarily a virtue, but achieving flexibility with a sentence is a stylistic asset. Sentence combining is another practical way of working on style.

Revision is also a conscious way of approaching style. It does not always have to be done individually. If students in a class are grouped in twos, they can talk about possible word choices and arrangements in their papers. They are doing several things important to the composing process: they are becoming critically aware, they are learning to verbalize certain intuitive responses they feel, and they are actually pinpointing details of the writing that make a difference in the total effect. This kind of cooperative revision is especially valuable if all students are obliged to begin by commending one or two details in the paper they are reading. Criticism and revision are so closely associated with negativism that we often ignore the fact that praise can be a major incentive to the writer for trying harder to please the reader.

Once students understand that producing a readable style is something within their control, not a God-given talent they

[8]See Kellogg W. Hunt, *Grammatical Structures Written at Three Grade Levels* (Urbana, Ill.: National Council of Teachers of English, 1965); "Syntactic Maturity in School Children and Adults," *Monographs of the Society for Research in Child Development*, Serial No. 134, Vol. 35, No. 3, 1970. Also John C. Mellon, *Transformational Sentence-Combining* (Urbana, Ill.: National Council of Teachers of English, 1969) and Frank O'Hare, *Sentence Combining* (Urbana, Ill.: National Council of Teachers of English, 1973).

may have been deprived of, they are likely to consider more carefully the choices they make, for style is ultimately a mingling of self and strategy.

REPRESENTATIVE PROJECTS

1. Since the capacity to write a long but readable sentence is one of the marks of a mature writer, sentence averages give students some notion how they perform in relation to other writers. Various studies have indicated that established writers average about twenty-one words per sentence. One has to realize immediately that averages obscure the range of variation. Sentences of forty-one words, ten words, and twelve words average twenty-one words per sentence, but so also do twenty-three, nineteen, and twenty-one. The effect of one group of sentences is undoubtedly quite different from the effect of the other group. Nevertheless, having students count the words in their sentences and average them is one way to demonstrate in what direction individual students need to move. A student who perhaps averages thirty-six words per sentence needs first of all to test the readability of the sentences and then to consider dividing some of them. On the other hand, a student who averages fifteen words per sentence has clearly something to learn about sentence development.

Other counts can be made: percentage of polysyllables and monosyllables, percentage of verbs in passive voice, percentage of sentences with subordinate clauses, etc. The danger in this kind of counting is that it may lead to misconceptions about style—that more is better or that 35 percent is desirable and 15 percent permissible. These kinds of quantification may obscure the fact that the ultimate test of prose is its readability and the ability of the reader to understand the writer's intentions. Statistics must be used with discretion.

2. Perhaps one of the simplest and most effective ways to test the felicity of a particular sentence is to read it aloud and to read it in the context of other sentences. Students who are able to hear the rhythms of a writer's prose and read it with skill are likely to have an inner ear for their own sentences. These statements assume that reading, especially oral reading, is one way to develop the intuitive senses. Students who routinely are required to read themes aloud in class will learn to test them in advance. If this technique seems too much like a public humiliation—as it sometimes is—then oral reading ought to be done as a part of a private conference. A student should be able to read his own prose or her own prose with ease. The prose should also permit the teacher to read it without stumbling or fumbling.

3. Have students choose five selections of nonfiction prose that to them clearly represent different prose styles. Have them observe the differences in the writing in terms of
   a. The purpose and occasion for writing
   b. The tone of voice or lack of voice
   c. The variety of usage
   d. The presence or absence of features like parallelism, repetition, metaphor, and similar rhetorical strategies.

4. More advanced students can be asked to set up a taxonomy of prose styles. The aim is to observe the characteristics and differences of various styles and to determine the basis of the classification system. Is it made on the basis of language, the audience addressed, the mode, or the purpose? In *Prose Styles: Five Primary Types* (Minneapolis: University of Minnesota Press, 1966), Huntington Brown discusses the deliberative style (persuasion), the expository style (treatise, lesson, sermon), the tumbling style (the instinctive expression of the speaker), the prophetic style (Biblical prophecy, stoic philosophy, the essay), and the

indenture style (legal documents, private formal messages). Have students invent their own terms.

The same objective of classifying and comparing styles can be accomplished by having students assemble a mini-anthology of five or six essays representing identifiable prose styles. They should then be asked to write an introduction to this collection explaining the characteristics and differences.

5. Reproduce three prose translations of the same passage from Homer's *Odyssey* (or a comparable work with multiple translations available). Compare the three, not in terms of their fidelity to the original, but in terms of their stylistic effects. How do they differ? What accounts for the differences?

6. Have students write ten variations of one of their own sentences. When they have finished, have them discriminate by marking the sentences as follows:

   B = the best one
   A = acceptable in some contexts
   M = clearly monstrous

7. Refer again to the discussion of the sense of the normative in Chapter 4 and to Wayne Booth's rhetorical stance in this chapter. Have students bring in examples of writing that to them are clearly "out of tune" with their normative values. Discuss the reasons. Are these reactions intuitively perceived or based on more conscious judgments?

13

Evaluation

Evaluation obviously implies values, but many teachers evaluate without defining them or just feel frustrated because they can't quantify the values they hold. Without clearly defined values, it is impossible to make consistent judgments and discriminations. And it is better yet if we can verbalize them so that commenting and grading do not seem personal without reference to objective criteria.

A number of years ago, when I was director of the freshman program at another university, I was once visited at the end of the semester by a steady stream of students from one instructor. All of them thought their grades for the course should be higher than they were. That complaint is not unusual in itself. Those who complain are not likely to be seeking a lower grade. In this case, however, the unusual numbers caused me to look into the situation. The outcome is fairly easy to explain.

A new instructor, quite desperate about the whole matter of grading, confessed that she really couldn't make discriminations about value and finally solved her problem by giving all of her students a C, hoping that the "average" grade would keep everyone happy. She was wrong, of course. The people who came to see me were the B and A students, who were not satisfied with less than they deserved.

After that extreme case, I realized that the director of the program had a responsibility to see that new instructors talked about values, because lacking a set of values they would tend to deal only with particular flaws. In *Principles of Literary Criticism*, I. A. Richards makes the point that "we pay attention to externals when we do not know what else to do with a poem."[1] The same is true of reading student papers. Not knowing what else to do, teachers proofread instead of reading critically. Thus, error-free writing becomes synonymous in the minds of students with good writing, but of course it isn't necessarily.

The vocabulary of writing teachers includes words like clarity, coherence, and conciseness. They are probably not very meaningful to students as abstract entities. They may be meaningful in terms of particular passages if the comments attempt to explain the difficulty, not simply label it with symbols like *Cl*, *Coh*, and *Con*. For instance, a passage like the following one needs a fairly extended comment if the instructor hopes to address the problem at all.

> When I see a dropout, I see a person who will fail all of his adult life. A person who quits the system because they think it is too tough but every time the person trys to get back in it will be harder and harder and that person will have to resort to something bad to try to break it, and those people are in jails all over this land and it is their own fault as soon as they get out of jail they will do something wrong and go right back. Most people who get welfare or other help are people who have dropped out of the rat race.
>
> *Comment to Student:* First of all, read your first sentence and your last one. Both of them are clear, direct statements. Then read the one in between. See if you can divide that long sentence into two or three short ones so that each one speaks as clearly as your other two sentences do.

---

[1] (New York: Harcourt, Brace and Co., 1948), p. 24.

This comment is an attempt to get the student to revise his writing in terms of a standard he sets for himself. He is able to write some good sentences. He has to recognize the difference between the good ones and the bad ones and try to perform consistently. I would further emphasize that I would not mark anything else, like "a person . . . they." In terms of the difficulty this student has with sentence recognition, the correction of "a person . . . they" seems like an unnecessary refinement at this stage.

As a matter of interest, note what adequate punctuation does for the same paragraph without any changes in word order. What appears to be a problem in sentence construction could be mainly a punctuation problem:

> When I see a dropout, I see a person who will fail all of his adult life—a person who quits the system because they think it is too tough. But every time the person trys to get back in, it will be harder and harder, and that person will have to resort to something bad to try to break it. And those people are in jails all over this land, and it is their own fault. As soon as they get out of jail, they will do something wrong and go right back. Most people who get welfare or other help are people who have dropped out of the rat race.

In some instances, the simplest way to comment is to demonstrate how much more directly something can be written. For the student who writes "I want to learn certain skills of which I have had no previous learning," I would simply underline the "of which" construction and substitute "that I have not previously learned." In most instances, students ought to be asked to come up with their own revisions, but here the problem is explaining what a circumlocution is. Certainly, labels like "awkward" or "idiom" would explain nothing, because the writer seems to think she is doing something right by not putting a preposition at the end of a sentence.

These particular comments emphasize the value of communication, the ability of the student to write something that someone else can understand. Yet we also judge the value of what is being communicated. A theme that begins "One of today's innumerable problems is a human one" has not initially communicated anything worth communicating. The sentence tells us something that is completely self-evident. The sentence does not inform because, as Kinneavy says, "A statement which is completely predictable carries no information.[2] A good bit of C-ish writing falls under the category of uninformative discourse. As teachers, we need to ask ourselves what a good idea is. Students tend to think a good idea is one the teacher agrees with. There should be more objective standards than that. When I read a sentence like the following, I see the possibilities of a good idea: "Crude, vindictive, insolent, and overcome by his own conceit, Jesus of Nazareth still laid the foundation of one of the world's most important theologies and systems of ethics." The sentence is striking; it is a bold assertion about the character of Jesus. But novelty itself does not make a good idea; it helps as a way of making a statement attractive, but a good idea cannot be just a flash. It has to be supportable. The abstract draws strength from the concrete; the general from the particular. We do not know whether insights are weak or strong until we are able to test them. And we can't actually judge whether the assertion about Jesus has value as an idea until we see the evidence. One of the striking differences between talking and writing is that spoken assertions are often not tested as written ones are. Spoken ones are accepted without support. Rarely is a written assertion simply accepted. It has to be established. It has to lead somewhere.

The capacity of an idea for development may be proportionate to the clarity of it in our own minds. Fuzzy notions are unproductive because they are tentative. They have not been analyzed, subjected to tests of logic, measured against experience, plumbed for depth. A good idea persists in the writer's mind and prevails over opposing views. It is persuasive.

A common theme assignment asks students to re-examine some idea that they have taken for granted, perhaps one commonly accepted in the home or community, perhaps something

---

[2]James L. Kinneavy, *A Theory of Discourse* (Englewood Cliffs, N.J.: Prentice-Hall, 1971), p. 93

like the belief that suicide is an act of cowardice. What they sometimes learn is that what seemed like a sound idea to start with does not stand the test of clarity under scrutiny. Seen in a full light, the idea diminishes in value.

We are aware that many ideas do not have absolute and continuing value. They are relative to particular times and contexts. Changing circumstances may demand a shift in what is considered sound. In 1969, colleges abandoned requirements right and left. That may have been a good idea in terms of expediency—a relevance to the social climate. In 1979, those same abandoned requirements are being restored. That may be a good idea in terms of the prevailing concept of education at a particular school—a relevance to humanistic goals. A good idea in one context cannot always prevail in another. In a day when the media draw the world closely together, we see that differences of cultural patterns account for many of the differences in value and may even create an inseparable barrier to understanding and agreement. An idea needs to be considered in the context in which it has been established.

Values such as informativeness, supportability, clarity, soundness, and relevance can be explained to students and illustrated. The value of an idea is not totally subjective. Once students learn to identify the qualities of ideas they consider good, they will learn that their own ideas are subject to similar standards.

But communication is only one value of writing. In writing, we seek certainty, lack of ambiguity, fullness of meaning, and effectiveness. These are values that depend upon *how* we write a thought in addition to *what* the thought is. The following example illustrates how tone can interfere with the writer's purpose:

> Although my utopia differs from More's, it also has relative similarities. There is always clean and crisp air, purified by the ocean breezes and Washington rain storms. Clean water is the *rule* rather than the *exception* as nearby the placid Willapa Bay, the awesome Columbia River, and tortuous rivers and meandering streams all join with the mighty Pacific Ocean. In these waters can be found one of the world's most bounteous supplies of game and food fish, as salmon, trout, perch,

cod, tuna, sturgeon, bass, crab, oysters, and clams make their homes there. On the heavily timbered lands game abounds and in the fertile fields crops flourish. In nearby forest elk, deer, bear, vermin, upland game birds, and water fowl are a common sight and during the proper seasons hunter success runs high. In the rich bottom lands crops of grain, cattle, fruit, vegetables and berries prosper in the mild Pacific coast climate.

Comment to student: Seems a bit too bounteous to be convincing. Is there a way to moderate the language and still get the same facts? Look at the adjectives. Look at the catalogues. Try another version.

If in this class there has been previous discussion of the writer's and reader's sense of the normative, which we discussed in Chapter 4, then this student is likely to understand why this comment has been made. It is an attempt to work for a tone that in turn works for the writer's purpose.

Drawing the line between substance and manner leads me to consider briefly the relation of other teachers in a school to the English teachers. One of the standing clichés of the business is that every teacher ought to be an English teacher. Indeed, true. But the essential differences in value never get resolved. English teachers insist that "rightness" include rightness of expression as well as rightness of meaning. Other teachers claim that they cannot penalize students for deficiencies in diction, tone, organization, and mechanics. Their attitude only reflects more widespread beliefs in the society as a whole, epitomized recently by J. Mitchell Morse in two sentences: "For just as those girls were expected to believe that athletic skill was unladylike, so we are all asked to believe, in this age of condescending pseudo-populism, that intellectual skill is un-American. We are asked to believe that slovenliness of speech and writing goes hand in hand with democratic virtue, and good grammar with effete intellectual snobbery."[3] There is more to Morse's statement than rhetorical flare. He characterizes the total context in which the English teacher works. The value system concerning the use of the language within the English classroom is

---

[3]"The Age of 'Logophobia,'" *The Chronicle of Higher Education*, 14 (May 16, 1977), 40.

clearly different from that outside. Outside, the primary value is communication. Inside, the aim is both effective and responsible communication.

As soon as we talk about better communication—about a value system based upon the manner in which the writing is produced—we return to the intuitive resources of the individual that are the main source of those values. They must be constantly reinforced by the comments teachers make. But what most characteristically happens when English teachers read student papers or, for that matter, when students read each other's papers? They find fault. Comment emphasizes what is wrong, not what is right. Major concern focuses on the limitations of the prose; the strengths are taken for granted. Yet many student writers continue to hobble along in crippled fashion because they have never learned what their strengths are. Even the more proficient writers share the insecurities of poor writers. They all fear that most of the time they are in jeopardy. Confident writers are extremely rare. People get discouraged in any activity if they find no satisfaction within themselves or gain no approval from others. If composition students derive no particular satisfaction from writing and, in addition, receive no encouragement from others, they cannot be expected to have enthusiasm for what they are learning and doing. Writing become onerous labor, without reward.

Comments like "Good," "Particularly striking," or simply "I like this" are often sufficient to get a grin of satisfaction from many students. Recently, on a brief assignment, I wrote at the bottom of a student's paper simply "Looks good." When I gave him his paper, he blurted out: "Look at that—just two words. Period." I thought he was complaining about the skimpy comment, whereupon he added, "It's the best comment I've received from anybody all quarter. Just two clear words. No qualifications." It is surprising at times what brevity will do. At other times, however, it is good to explain why a sentence works, on the assumption that students may not know, or if they do, they can then be assured that the instructor is tuned to some of the subtleties they are attempting.

Student Sentence: I am affected socially in a number of ways. First of all, I inherit the image of a drug user and criminal: lazy, untrustworthy, irresponsible, unkempt and dirty, unintelligent and generally worthless. *Marginal Comment:* I like the way you vary the series. So much better than just a list of adjectives.

SS: The ring is as small as a dollar bill, but at the sound of the bell its value becomes a mint [description of a championship boxing match]. MC: Second part of sentence has an element of surprise. Makes the point well.

SS: No roofs ever get fixed. Surely no one fixes a roof when it's raining, and when it's not raining, who needs to? That's human nature. MC: About as compact as expression can get. Nice edge of humor.

SS: Strindberg's *The Ghost Sonata* is not a play written to fill one's heart with hope for human triumph over the "labor of keeping the dirt of life at a distance," as the girl aptly phrases the problem. Instead, Strindberg destroys the false dreams of the romantic and, through a horror-filled nightmare, shows the blackness of reality that is hidden so securely behind a well-scrubbed facade of deceit. This is shown symbolically by the house—modern, pleasant-appearing, so seemingly filled with "beauty and elegance." It is a mansion. To the passerby it is the home of virtuous and high-minded aristocrats: the wealthy colonel, the benevolent consul, the aged spinster, the baron, the beautiful daughter, and the well-mannered servants. But what are these people after Mr. Hummel, the most flagrant deceiver of them all, disrupts their stagnating existence, and "the deepest secret is divulged—the mask torn from the imposter, the villain exposed. . . ."? All of these people are tortured by the sins of their past; all live on in the horrid loneliness of a hell full of "crime and deceit and falseness of every kind," in which payment is painfully wrung from their condemned souls. MC: Particularly smooth working of quotations into your own prose.

SS: [Commentary on a TV commercial featuring Mrs. Olson plugging Folger's coffee.] Get rid of Mrs. Olson! Replace her with a man in a gorilla suit, drop an anvil on his head, and have a midget say, "Drink Folgers." MC: Just ludicrous enough for this kind of parody.

SS: In a fictional but probable story written for a popular girls' magazine, a school principal posted these rules: "Boys shall not wear bluejeans or long hair; girls shall wear skirts and blouses or dresses, but no pants of any kind." As a result, boys showed up in shorts and white jeans. The girls complained to their parents that the principal would not allow them to wear underpants. The unhappy principal relented by allowing students to dress as they wanted to.

MC: Amusing illustration, although not highly probable. Good concise summary of the story.

Praise of praising as a way of commenting on student papers is sometimes dismissed as Pollyannish nonsense. If *praise* is too strong a word to apply to student writing, substitute *reinforcement* or *commendation* or *approval*—anything of a constructive nature. And let the tone be positive without the inevitable *but*— "essentially novel idea, but . . . ," taking away with one hand what the other gives.

Does the psychology of reinforcement really need to be argued if we are going to try to educate large numbers of students to be proficient writers? It should be the major resource of every writing teacher. It should be practiced whenever it can be done honestly and ungrudgingly. If a paper is filled with errors, some teachers do not want to give it any kind of favorable recognition. That may be a mistake. On the other hand, it may also be a way of saying—and it should be said upon occasion—that the interferences to communication are too great to know whether something deserves a compliment or not. Too often, however, errors are used as an excuse for saying nothing positive.

Is praise enough, however?

By all means, encouragement must come first as a way of gaining the confidence of students and giving them confidence in what they are doing. They must see that their reader-critic is capable of recognizing and acknowledging that something in the writing has worked. If something hasn't worked, then we usually need an outsider to tell us. Self-criticism is fine as far as it goes, but it cannot go far enough to get us completely outside ourselves. All professionals whose work is being judged by accepted standards of excellence need someone to comment critically on their performance. Characteristically, this will be someone knowledgeable and someone whom they respect.

If a teacher is knowledgeable and if students respect that teacher, not for knowledge alone, but for the common interest they share in making the writing as good as the students can make it, then the teacher can begin to point out weaknesses, not ten or fifteen flaws at once, but one or two, because, psychologically, we cannot cope with a deluge of our deficiencies. The tone of corrective comments is all important. In this regard, a beginning teacher also needs an outsider—another teacher—to react to comments that have been written on student papers. In turn, the new teacher needs to read comments by other teachers to test what kinds of reactions those trigger. A student's attitude toward the teacher will be strongly influenced by the tone of the remarks. A good bit can be accomplished by questions and suggestions that honestly ask the student to rethink an idea or reconsider a phrasing, at the same time implying that what has been written does not quite come off. Here are student sentences (SS) and possible marginal comments (MC) that are intended to pinpoint weaknesses and suggest inprovements.

SS: I have never met a person who is perfect; nor have I met one who is thoroughly wicked. For I know only gray people—no black people, no white. For, in my opinion, all people are morally tainted, to a certain extent, varying with the individual. *Honoré de Balzac doesn't seem to uphold my theory.*

MC: Which way is it? Balzac doesn't agree with you? Or you don't agree with Balzac? Or, possibly, you don't find support in Balzac's novels?

SS: Grandpa Joad was as hard as they come. He was what you might call *hillbillyistic.*

MC: Say this word out loud. Do you still like it?

SS: [Opening of a theme] There is at present a surfeit of unwarrented adverse criticism of financially successful practitioners of the arts. For the purpose of a brief discussion, one or two examples from the arts of literature and music will suffice.

There seems to be an attitude among critics of the various arts that an artist cannot be financially successful and at the same time retain his artistic integrity. It is quite possible for this to happen, but it does not have to happen. A few examples help to make this evident.

MC: Paragraph 2 is a simpler, more direct statement of Paragraph 1. Why not make it the opening and drop the first?

SS: We have all heard woesome tales of maidens during the Middle Ages who pined away for their loves, who either died or *just walked out on them.*

MC: Why not get mileage out of this colloquial expression by giving it a mediaeval flavor: "or just rode out on them"?

> SS: My brain is exercised constantly by homework; I have *an accomplished feeling* after completing it.
> MC: Same as "a sense of accomplishment"?
>
> SS: The people after the earthquake did heroic deeds. The majority stayed and dug out from the debris, but there were some that packed and left. The valley was restored to normal about three months later. Even three months later the earth would tremble at times. The people came back with spirit and high morale. They helped each other. They began to live at a normal pace once more. They had won against the forces of nature.
> MC: Good opportunity for sentence combining. Give me a four-sentence version of the same paragraph without loss of significant detail.

Commenting on papers in the early stages requires patience and restraint because we have to suppress our usual tendency to attack weaknesses. Some teachers want to prove how tough they are; others, that they have high standards. Neither has to be preached or proved. Rigor and standards result from the expectations that are set on a day-by-day basis. Students also learn that they have to set standards for themselves. Not just anything scribbled during the last 20 minutes before class will be good enough if that kind of work meets with general indifference. The object of student writing should be, as it is in professional writing, to solicit approval, not to avoid failure. Success therefore depends upon approval.

Grades are not very successful in indicating approval simply because they are too generalized. Even in a graded class, grades should not be used during the time that a teacher is trying to establish a good working relationship with students. A failing grade on the first theme only perpetuates the discouragement that has gone before. Do we need to prove each time to particular students that they are starting once more from zero? The indication that they are even at "zero + 1" might provide enough incentive to move some of them along one more step, and then another, and then maybe a leap—if the teacher believes there is hope and continues to emphasize what has improved, not to stress always what remains to be done.

Using grades to register progress leads to the unfortunate habit of deliberately keeping early grades low so that there is somewhere for the student to go. Students expect progress to be registered continuously by gradations, although the teacher may soon reach a ceiling grade. What happens then? Do B's move to A's simply because a theme is better than the previous one, although it is far short of excellence? The solution, as I have already indicated, is not to grade early papers at all, and from that point on to grade occasionally to let students know, as they say, "where they stand."

Theoretically, Pass/Fail grading (which usually turns out to be Pass/Pass) or Credit/No Credit is an ideal arrangement for writing courses because the focus shifts from the grade to the comment. In the systems I have known, Pass in the Pass/Fail arrangement includes all grades from A to D. Credit in the C/NC arrangement represents C and above. The difficulty with equating nongraded systems with grades is that teachers must still think in traditional terms. It is difficult at the present to escape the grading system, even when the symbols are removed.

But something can happen in the classroom if the preoccupation with grades—C instead of D, A instead of B+ —is diminished. The grade is less of a threat; accordingly, students are less inclined to play safe. They often show improvement because they dare more. We are all familiar with people who substitute simple words that they can spell for more appropriate but difficult words they can't spell. The same is true of sentence structure and other stylistic elements that require the writer to be more venturesome, but also more vulnerable. Of primary importance in the ungraded class, however, is the fact that assessment is made by the comment alone, not by the grade plus a comment. No student can be fooled by an encouraging comment and a failing grade. Grades categorize. An E is an E, and the idea of high failure is not likely to meet with widespread acceptance. But comments on an ungraded paper can tactfully indicate degrees of improvement that grades cannot register even when the scale is extended to include pluses and minuses.

Despite the favorable setting for improvement that exists in an ungraded writing class, a word of caution should be added about the difference between the ungraded class in theory and the ungraded class in practice. The first major obstacle is that students are hopelessly grade-conditioned. Many of them act as if their progress in writing depends upon seeing C+ change to B− and then to B, although those gradations may indicate no reasons for the improvement. The second obstacle is the low priority students give the Pass/Fail writing class, particularly if it is the only ungraded class in their program. At special times during the term, usually when tests are given in other classes, college students will skip classes or, if they come, not prepare class assignments. These are not insurmountable obstacles, however. They must simply be anticipated and countered in some way by the ingenuity of the instructor.

Graded classes predominate throughout the country in both high schools and colleges. Every teacher therefore ought to be able to handle grades responsibly. If it is true that grades are often meaningless, then we should make serious efforts to make them meaningful.

First of all, grades that represent categories like Honors, Excellent, and Average or superior, above average, and average—evaluations based upon comparative standards—are not particularly meaningful in a writing class. At least, they can't mean very much to an individual student who lacks the perspective to know what "average"means. And they can't mean very much either to a beginning instructor who has not read enough student papers to know what "average" is.

For a writing class, the most useful definitions I have found are those used by the College Entrance Examination Board for Advanced Placement examinations. If we can equate their five-part numbering system with letter grades, we get the following scale:

> A—Demonstrates unusual competence
> B—Demonstrates competence
> C—Suggests competence
> D—Suggests incompetence
> E—Demonstrates incompetence

Obviously, the whole approach depends upon some recognizable standard of competence. That will vary, of course, but it doesn't have to vary so much among a group of teachers in the same course that one of them will give an essay a B and another will give the same essay an E. If that happens, one is enforcing eccentric values. In describing the qualifications of a good critic, I. A. Richards includes the following criterion: "He must be adept at experiencing, without eccentricities, the state of mind relevant to the work of art he is judging."[4] Eccentricity of judgment results when an instructor ignores completely one or more of the elements we have defined in the makeup of writing: the content, the form, the diction, the mechanics, and the style. Some instructors insist upon grading on content alone. The only important thing to them is *what the writer says*. For purposes of grading, I see this as an eccentricity of critical judgment. Others will give top priority to correctness. When I began as a teaching assistant in college English, the only instructions we were given about grading were to count two comma splices, two fragments, or five misspelled words as automatic E's. We then made our own individual scales: one comma splice, C; three misspelled words, C; one fragment and three misspelled words, E. Grading in this fashion was extremely simple. It required no critical judgment whatsoever. What it said to the student in effect was that the accurate use of mechanics was the most important value in writing. That too was an eccentricity of judgment.

By all means, evaluation must take into account all of the factors that can be judged in the final written version. That means performance should be graded, not the person; the effect, not the effort; the writing, not the writer. Evaluating an essay cannot be reduced to mathematical averaging, but it can become a process in which various elements of the writing are considered.

The beginning assumption of the teacher is important. Is each paper a C until it gets better or worse? Or is every paper potentially an A until for some reason or other it moves out of that range? Instructors who begin with the C-assumption often find themselves giving A's rather grudgingly, for an A becomes a

[4]*Principles of Literary Criticism*, p. 114

pinnacle, the acme of perfection. The A grade ought to represent a range, as all other grades do, perhaps not as wide as some
of the others if we are going to give serious recognition to the
word *unusual* ("Demonstrates unusual competence"), but a
range nevertheless.

If every paper is potentially an A until something happens
to it, then an instructor ought to be able to account for any
lower grade. Sometimes it takes no more than one sentence for
something drastic to happen. A student who in the first sentence
tells the reader, "Offensive aspects of a commercial that is particularly disliked by me only briefly describes my personal emotions on the subject" has plummeted. Exactly where is not yet
certain, and the lapse should not be considered fatal. Even
though the theme begins badly, it can recover along the way,
but clearly the A is lost in the first sentence because in no sense
can the competence, if that is eventually established, be considered unusual. (Unusually bad doesn't count.) In this instance,
what has to be established before this theme is completed is the
degree of competence.

What, then, is competence? Or, in terms of grades, how
can we characterize a B-paper that, according to our value scale,
demonstrates competence?

Before attempting some description, I must confess that
through the years, as I have tried to collect essays in various
grade categories for practice grading, I have always found difficulty picking representative B-papers or, to put the matter another way, finding essays that most of the graders agreed were B-
papers. At first, they seem to think that a B-essay is marked by a
kind of undistinguished flawlessness. In actuality, a B-essay may
have both distinctive features and flaws, but the flaws are not so
numerous or serious as to throw doubt upon the proficiency of
the writer. Perhaps the clearest difference between the C-writer
and the B-writer is that the B-writer seems to be in control of
the writing. It doesn't just happen. It has purpose, direction, and
strategy. The clearest difference between the B-writer and the A-
writer is that the A-writer often brings intellectual and imaginative resources to the task of writing that transform the material

and language in some unusual way. That quality comes through clearly. In fact, in evaluating an essay, some graders want to recognize only that quality, ignoring the problems the writer may have with structure or clarity or punctuation.

Despite the fact that B is too often defined relatively—not as good as A, better than C—a number of positive statements can be made in terms of the five major components of writing we have discussed.

B-ESSAY

Content

The material of a B-essay shows some sign of independent thought and gives evidence of the writer's active engagement with the topic. The writer may make an enlightening comparison or show some relationship that is not immediately apparent to the reader. In brief, something illuminating is said. But illumination need not be thought of as something new, only as something presented in such a way that the reader sees it anew. In a speech made at a writing conference in 1977, E. D. Hirsch, Jr. said (I quote him from my own notes), "You cannot possibly write better than you can read." That capacity to read with understanding and to penetrate beneath the obvious becomes the basis of the differences in content of A, B, and C papers, even if these essays are not directly about reading materials.

Form

B-writers ordinarily show a clear sense of order, although they may not be totally successful in working out the plan set forth or implied at the beginning. Frequently, one point will be fully developed and two or three others skimpily treated. The paragraphing thus appears to deteriorate, although such flaws in development may be more a result of the word limit set for a theme or the limitations of time a student has to prepare an academic assignment. We have to recognize that the 500-word essay is a relatively tight structure that does not allow much opportunity for leisurely discourse.

On the whole, however, B-students are conscious of planning and tailor their material to relate to the central point. With this kind of formal control, the essays show evidence of transitions and of thematic and verbal echoes that hold the thoughts together.

Diction

B-students, like A-students also, have developed a lexicon that gives them a sense of freedom with the language simply because they have more words to work with than less capable students. From one paper graded B, I record five words that I would not normally expect in a typical C paper: *purport, expound, jeopardized, myriad,* and *scholastic.* They are all accurately used; they are all well used in context. They are not exactly what we would consider big words or exotic words. They are, however, essentially "literate" words—words that we absorb from reading rather than listening. B-students, in comparison with A-students, may seem just a bit prosaic in their use of words simply because they shy away from the flamboyant choice, the inventive coinage, or the striking metaphor.

Mechanics

It is more difficult to generalize about mechanics than about almost any of the other factors. The best of students are sometimes notoriously indifferent to punctuation and capitalization, as if these were the concern only of teachers and editors, ignoring of course the fact that those most concerned are actually readers, who must decipher and interpret when mispunctuation or the lack of punctuation misleads. Nevertheless, B-students tend to turn in clean, correct papers. In fact, as a group, they may be better able to explain why they have done what they have done than A-students.

Style

Consistent with their accuracy in mechanics, B-students also show clear control of the grammar. Verbs agree with subjects and pronouns with antecedents; tense and person are maintained with consistency. In brief, there are few interferences to the thought.

Yet, if this description seems to suggest only that B-students are safe writers, it should be noted that most of them are aware of rhetorical strategies and can often use devices like parallelism, repetition, contrast, and the rhetorical question with effect. Mature use of subordination permits them to write a compact and varied style.

B-students may be less egocentric or eccentric than A-students, but their individuality becomes evident in their use of detail and illustration and in their capacity to assume a position that they can assert and defend. B-writers indeed are often confident, disciplined writers, wondering why their best efforts still fall short of top quality. That can be explained finally only by seeing what the best student writers are capable of doing.

For some tangible evidence of these generalizations, here is a student essay of B-quality. It was written during a 50-minute class period, a completely impromptu assignment based upon several quotations. This student chose the Johnson quotation that surfaces at the end. The running commentary on this essay is similar to the kinds of thoughts that might occur to a reader in the process of commenting and grading, although all of these reactions obviously would not be recorded or result in actual comment to the student. (In all of the samples, spelling errors are reproduced.)

Progress—A Direct Result of Curiosity

The first few years of life are those in which we learn the most. A child is curious and his curiosity leads him to make many investigations. These investigations teach him many things about the world around him. Watching a small child toddle around the room can be an enlightening experience. He approaches an object and examines it thoroughly. He smells it, shakes it, and tastes it. He drops it to see if it will break or bounce. He's testing this object. He wants to know what it is, what it does, how it does it. The conclusions he draws as a result of this testing may be naive, but his method is the same as that of the most sophisticated scholar or scientist.

It is the method of questioning. Why does this object do this? Does it always react in this way? Is there anything I can do to change the normal reaction? What? Man uses this method every day; this method enables him to learn.

Learning then is a direct result of questioning. In other words, learning is a direct result of being curious. Curiosity is important to progress. It stimulates the mind to investigate and by investigating the mind learns new facts. Using these facts the mind reaches new conclusions and progress is the result.

All progress can be traced to a curious mind at work. All great discoveries began with a question. If the world is flat, thought Columbus, why do the sails disappear at the horizon? Why, asked Newton, does an apple fall to the ground? The curiosity of men like these led to subsequent investigations and these investigations led to more knowledge about man's environment.

In a world void of curiosity, man's development would cease. There could be no progress. If no one questioned the present state of things, there would be no new facts learned. No changes would be made and civilization would stagnate.

Curiosity is then as Samuel Johnson said "one of the permanent and certain characteristics

First three sentences: Unnecessary throat-clearing opening. Perhaps better dropped or combined into one sentence.
Sentence 4 could be the opening. Concrete, vivid. Short phrases catch the spirit of the scene. Good use of parallel structure. Writer seems to know what she is doing. First paragraph ends up with significant point. (Anyone especially concerned about the use of the generic "he" might point out that this paragraph works just as well by changing "child" to "children" and changing the "he's" consistently to "they's.")
Paragraph 2: Another good paragraph that illustrates the "method of questioning" by asking questions. The thought moves forward.
Paragraph 3: The conclusion of the first two paragraphs effectively stated as a transition and clearly pointed by "then." Remainder of paragraph restates and develops the thought.
Paragraph 4: Specific examples, although not especially striking.

Final two paragraphs represent a falling off in the development of the thought, leading to an ineffectual ending. Johnson's quotation unnecessarily elaborated upon. It should be noted, of a vigorous mind." A man with a vigoro.is mind progresses. He questions his surroundings and learns by questioning. A man with a dull mind does not progress. He questions nothing and learns nothing. He is void of curiosity and he stagnates.

however, that the building to the quotation at the end indicates the forethought that went into the essay. Most students writing on an assignment of this kind begin with the quotation.

In terms of these generalizations based on innumerable papers with B grades, we may summarize by saying that demonstrated competence in writing represents:

1. An ability to absorb ideas and experience and to interpret them meaningfully in a context of the writer's own conception.
2. A capacity to develop an idea with a clear sense of order.
3. A capacity to draw upon words adequate to express the writer's own thoughts and feelings.
4. An ability to use mechanics as an integral part of the meaning and effect of the prose.
5. A capacity to consider alternate ways of expression as a means of making stylistic choices possible.

A-ESSAY

It is a mistake to assume that an A-essay is everything a B-essay is and something more. In fact, an A-essay is not infrequently something less in terms of some of the factors. There may be less control on the part of the writer, less patience with detail, greater daring; and hence, upon occasion, greater bathos. The A-writer risks more and thus gains more or loses more depending upon the success of the venture. It seems appropriate, therefore, not to think of the qualities of the A-essay as magnifications of those of the B-essay, but to think of them separately as qualities of another species altogether. Any student with motivation and practice is capable of becoming a B-student. Not all of them, however, are capable of becoming A students. When a student becomes an A-writer, some new realization has occurred to that person. The individual views writing in different terms. What, then, are characteristics of A-writing?

Content

The first mark of the A-paper is that it invites reading. The author has something to say, or, if the topic is discouragingly barren, the writer finds a way of making something of nothing, either by humor or irony or fantasy. I have actually seen amusing and readable essays on the most hackneyed of all theme topics: What Did You Do Last Summer? Faced with a topic of that kind, the A-student will typically fail to take it seriously, recognize it as a pitfall and attempt to meet the challenge.

The A-student is one who never loses completely a sense of self in treating a subject. In fact, the subject is usually shaped in terms of the self. The egocentric is strong in the prose; the voice is identifiable. Note the whimsical treatment of an ordinary occurrence in the following opening of a theme, which bears all of the marks of A-writing:

> Running alongside our house is a cement path that leads to the garage. On one side stands a six-foot fence, and on the other towers a thorny hedge. This hedge happens to be a particularly healthy specimen—so healthy in fact that last summer I noticed it was becoming increasingly difficult to get past it without being soundly slapped by a branch. I considered trimming it back, but when I considered the work involved I decided to perfect my duck-and-weave technique instead. Besides, summer was almost over and everybody knows plants stop growing in the winter. Right?
>
> Wrong. I had failed to reckon with the malicious determination of that hedge. It simply would not stop growing. The old duck-and-weave technique didn't seem to work anymore. When I ducked, the hedge ducked; when I dodged, Hedge dodged. If I didn't know better, I might have sworn the overgrown weed was out to get me.

In the penultimate sentence, the hedge changes to Hedge, who from that point on becomes an arch-rival. The remainder of the essay narrates the bloody "arm-to-branch combat" until "an hour later, dead and dying branches littered the walkway." After the fury of the struggle, the author reflects: "Putting my clippers away, I went into the house feeling somehow that I had lost more than I won." In that sentence, the author distances himself from his own clever narrative and adds a subtle touch of ironic reflection. Other writers could possibly have brought off the battle description. This writer, however, sees in it a micro-cosm of more momentous struggles. This is the independent view that gives the essay an unusual quality and makes it worth an A.

Essentially what I have described in this student is a capac-ity to observe and reflect. The A-student sees possibilities for writing in almost any experience and has the capacity to draw upon both reading and experience for details and examples. As a result, the content of A-writing is often fertile, leading to diverse interpretations and richness of meaning. These are the marks of mature prose.

Form

A-writers, characteristically confident writers, although not necessarily disciplined writers, are more likely to depend on their intuitive resources than less skilled writers. Generalizations therefore are difficult because there are more flexibilities. An A-student, for instance, is likely to let an essay shape itself in the course of writing rather than plan it in a preliminary outline. The success or failure of the development, especially the para-graphing, therefore, has to be judged on its purpose and appro-priateness. A writer with a good rhythmic sense will perceive the ebb and flow of generalization and particularity in the develop-ment of a thought, will know the importance of ending as well as beginning, will recognize where emphasis is needed. These can all be indicated by paragraphing that has a rhetorical rather than a strictly logical basis. Failure on the part of the teacher to recognize irregular patterns of paragraphing as intentional may be a failure to recognize the writer's attempt to interpret the material. On the other hand, erratic development needs to be recognized, for it represents a lack of a perceptible plan.

Diction

The most characteristic feature of the language of an A-paper is the individuality and aptness of the diction. A-writers

write their own words, not someone else's; that is, they free
themselves as much as possible from clichés and jargon in an
effort to inject a freshness into their prose. They are concerned
with expressiveness as well as clear communication. They therefore do not shy away from the apt metaphor, sensory detail, or
the striking phrase. When I read, "The silence of Samburan
creates an atmosphere of palpable expectancy," I recognize a
writer who reveals sensitivity to language, who knows how to
choose and arrange words.

A-writers are not only willing to use a literate vocabulary;
they are often overanxious to a fault, falling into a pompous,
polysyllabic style. The familiar injunction never to use a big
word when a small one will do does not particularly help the A-
student, who actually needs to learn when "big" words can be
appropriately used. Big or small then becomes a stylistic choice.

Mechanics

Mechanics in A-writing are generally acceptable, not always because the writers can explain syntactically what they are
doing, but because they have a good ear that intuitively leads
them to make right choices. If there is any tendency in punctuation, it is to overpunctuate rather than underpunctuate in order to keep fairly involved sentences moving smoothly.

Since chronic misspelling ordinarily has nothing to do with
intelligence, students who are unusually competent in other regards may be wretched spellers. Such cases must be treated individually in terms of grades. Certainly failing a student because
of misspelling who otherwise shows unusual competencies is not
going to solve the spelling problem.

Style

Most A-writers in high school and the early college years
have already developed an identifiable style. They are fluent.
They know how to control sentences for rhetorical purposes.
They use their intuitive senses to create effects that not only

emphasize meaning but evoke reaction. If they wish, they are capable of changing voices. To them, style is like a musical instrument that can produce a variety of effects if they know their instrument and its parts and know that it must be kept under control to do what they want to do.

Perhaps the most marked characteristic of A-students is their inability to suppress the personal voice, whether it emerges through the vocabulary, the metaphors, the uniqueness of viewpoint, or any other quality that announces the individuality of the writer. But this is not unique, because some unskilled writers, especially minority students, show the same capacity to use language boldly and imaginatively and to assume a highly individualized point of view. The lack of skill in these writers is often a lack of control over the material—an inability to produce intentionally the effects they want and to consider the choices they make in terms of alternatives. Typical A-students have developed some critical acumen. They want to put something down in the best possible way and often show a reluctance to accept criticism that suggests a particular word or sentence might be improved. This pride—this protectiveness of the phrase—is one of the qualities that make their writing unusual in the first place.

A-writers characteristically have something worthwhile to say. If the point of departure for writing is a reading assignment, they will clearly show their advantage by reading perceptively and often responding in terms of other things they have read. Thus, as superior readers, they show maturity in their ideas and reinforce their own opinions by reference to specific facts and concrete examples.

Additionally, A-students will often show unusual capacities by simply assuming the least expected angle of vision upon a subject. It will occur to them upon occasion to look at the world upside down through their legs. What they see is therefore unexpected; what they write is therefore fresh.

Instead of choosing an A-paper based on literature that invites a standard kind of critical prose, I have picked one based on personal experience, a subject that any student might select, but one that in this instance is particularly well treated.

Rows of moored fishing boats slipped behind us as we chugged slowly out of the harbor. We had come to the Mexican coastal village of Puerto Penasco two days before to go deep sea fishing, and at last we were on our way. Tilted back in my chair at the rear of the boat I watched the dirty colored sea gulls swoop angrily around us screeching indignantly at being disturbed.

We had nearly reached the end of the harbor, and a panoramic view of the surrounding countryside spread out before us. It was easy to see why the town was called Rocky Point in translation. Low rolling hills covered with cacti and desert shrubs came almost to the sea; and then, as if the top layers of the earth had been scraped away, barren gray rocks slanted down into the water. Sharp points of slimy rock thrust their way out of the shallows all along the coast. Perched precariously on the rough rocks and land edging the sea, the ramshackle Mexican village dozed peacefully in the sun. Shrimpboats of every size, shape, and description lay on their sides on the mud flats. These boats were being overhauled and prepared for the town's real industry, shrimp fishing, later in the year. On the very edge of the cliff jutting out over the water, the pink and cream colored ultramodern hotel looked out of place amidst all the beat-up little buildings of the village. The hotel had been built for a political meeting during World War II and was now being operated by an American couple as a resort.

Finally we reached the open sea, and the boat rose and fell regularly as the long ocean waves rocked it. The water, which had been green in the harbor, began changing to a light blue. The farther we went from shore, the deeper the blue became. Far behind us the land began fading into a silvery mist. The rough and unwelcoming coastline softened into an inviting sheen of soft color. All around us the water heaved and roared. Our wake swept behind us like white frothy lace. Only the water was left to be seen by this time as the land had long been left behind. All that could be seen were the boat, ourselves, and the sky. It was even hard to tell just where the ocean ended and

A fine opening that immediately impresses the reader with the writer's command of language and adds an imaginative touch that sets an expectation for what is to come.

Paragraph 2 maintains the quality of description, both in detail and choice of words.

Note the skillful use of alliteration in the sentence beginning "Sharp points of slimy rock . . . ." The description of the hotel at the end provides a contrast to the ruggedness of nature and sparseness of life among the villagers. The writer maintains a panoramic view.

Focus returns to the boat and the figures in Paragraph 1. The movement of the boat is described in terms of changing colors. The contrast in the final sentence again incorporates the two elements consistently developed throughout the description—the harshness and the beauty, the struggle and the peace.

the sky began. Everything seemed to be a deep
and unending blue stretching out in all directions
endlessly. The sun, hard and bright, beat down
mercilessly; but the ocean breeze swept over us
cooling and refreshing.

In terms of generalizations we have been making about A-
papers, we may summarize by saying that unusual competence
in writing represents:

1. An ability to avoid the obvious and thus gain insights that are
   personal and often illuminating.
2. A capacity to develop ideas flexibly and fluently, yet with control and purpose.
3. A special concern for the *bon mot*, even if it entails coining a
   word that the language does not provide.
4. An ability to use punctuation rhetorically, using it for effect as
   well as for clarity.
5. A willingness to be inventive with words and structures in order to produce a clearly identifiable style, even though at
   times the efforts may be too deliberate or fall short of the
   writer's intentions.

C-ESSAY

Even though our basic definition characterizes a C-paper as
one that "suggests competence" and therefore might embryoni-
cally include elements we have noted in B- and A-papers, we can
nevertheless point to other recurring characteristics that identify
these papers.

Content

Writers of C-papers may not be less fluent than writers of
better papers, but they make words count for less. The writing
may be padded and repetitious. The tendency to keep the
thought on a high level of generality without reference to detail
or specific illustrations causes the writing to seem thin. A paper
may be filled with truisms and hearsay evidence, with little indi-

cation of the writer's intellectual involvement with the subject. Thus, in writing about a reading assignment, summary will predominate over analysis. Quotations will be plentiful, but seldom integrated; they are used to fill out the word requirement. The surest mark of the C-paper is the preponderance of self-evident statements—all true, probably clearly and correctly phrased, but predictable and often trivial. Except for a dangling modifier, it is difficult to fault the following passage on its diction or sentence structure; it is nevertheless dull writing because it is completely obvious.

> A boarding school is a great asset to someone who is planning to go to college because it brings that person into contact with other students who come from different parts of the world and who have different characters and personalities. A school of this type teaches a boy how to live with other boys, and a feeling of a small community is established. Besides learning how to live with others, a boarding school still offers concentrated, supervised study and close individual attention from the instructor. These preparatory schools teach the student what to expect in college life, and I can truthfully say that I have benefited greatly from the advantages which these schools had to offer.

Form

Most C-writers will reveal that they are aware of organization, but to them form is formulaic. If some teacher has taught them the five-part essay beginning with an Introduction and ending with a Conclusion they will be committed to it, because they can make it work. And if they can make it work successfully, the arrangement may be a strength in the writing. In many instances, however, even though students have a workable skeletal frame, they have difficulty filling in the internal supports. They will state generalizations without support. A paragraph will go nowhere. They will move from one topic to another without transition. The essay as a whole therefore seems directionless. Many C-students characteristically are unable to think of form as setting a direction for thought or as setting expectations for the reader. An essay may simply wander.

Diction

At this point, perhaps we should emphasize that the writing in a C-paper is not uniformly weak. More characteristically, it is a combination of strengths and weaknesses. Seldom, however, does diction tend to be one of the strengths. A writer with little to say will try to fill out the page with words. And those words are frequently the first ones that come to mind. C-writing therefore depends strongly upon the cliché. The opening paragraph of this theme illustrates the tendency:

> There are many useful purposes in writing good fiction. The author may try to get his point across by using satire or comedy or serious drama. He may be ridiculing society or supporting a moral issue. But fiction accomplishes a goal many authors never realize. It offers the reader a golden opportunity to escape the problems and pressures of everyday life.

Lapses into jargon, slang or colloquialisms often lead to vacillations in tone and to unintentional humor. The following writer's attempt to consider seriously the smile on the face of the Mona Lisa is defeated completely by the limitations of the writer's language. In fact, if we consider all of the components, this writing falls well below C-level:

> To many different people I am sure that the Mona Lisa's smile suggests many different things, and to some people the smile proberly means nothing.
> To me the smile really doesn't mean any special one thing, but a few things. For example the smile could mean that she is happy and thats all. It could also mean that she likes Leo and she has these little thoughts creeping around in her little mind that after he has finished painting her. She wants to get a little party going, a very little party with just Leo and herself. Sure most people would or might say "but people back then didn't think about things like that," but people are only human. Even way back then.

The diction of the C-writer may perhaps be best explained as a lack of range. That may mean, in some cases, a minimal but workable vocabulary. In others, it may represent a deficiency that will continue to keep the writing undistinguished until the writer has more verbal resources to work with.

Mechanics

Many C-papers are perfectly correct in spelling and punctuation and capitalization. These are productive skills in composition, as we described them in Chapter 3. Almost anyone with an awareness of the basic structures of the language—the word, the phrase, the clause, and the sentence—should be able to use punctuation with a high degree of accuracy. Those who use it erratically, whether they are A- or C-students, seem to think of marks as condiments that can be sprinkled about with equal effectiveness wherever they fall. Yet those same writers will not dispense with them altogether. Faulty punctuation, like bad spelling, often has its source in the writer's own attitude. As we have already noted, correct use of mechanics is not a sure measure of value, but writers who are interested in excellence will always recognize that correctness is also a part of effectiveness.

Style

As writers learn that the language is highly flexible, that variety is infinite, and invention unbounded, they can expect their writing to show signs of individual identity. C-writers are often still struggling with fairly basic elements, like words and sentences. Thus, they lack a feeling of ease with language. Much C-writing is writing in the Plain Style, and the Plain Style is a safe style. Without any inspiration behind it, it is a perfunctory style. The following passage is typical of much C-writing:

> None of us has any doubt of the fact that there are many students in college that cheat. This is amazing to me because the results of cheating are good arguments to use against it. To go to school costs the student time and money, so it seems logical that he would want to make use of these things. Also, the student must lose his self-respect as well as the respect of others.

Everything is correct, including a singular verb *has* to agree with *none*. The opening is self-evident. The second sentence assumes a colloquial tone that in the following sentence leads the writer to connect two sentences with *so* instead of subordinating the first. (We usually talk that way.) The fourth sentence seems tagged on as an afterthought. It is difficult to respond to this prose in any way except indifference. It doesn't move the reader to outrage or indignation. It doesn't stir any interest. It doesn't set up any expectations. It doesn't raise any questions. Good prose isn't required to do these particular things, but it ought to do something, and this passage doesn't, essentially because it is lifeless writing. Writing of this kind makes the composition teacher's lot "not a happy one."

In terms of generalizations we have been making about C-papers, we may summarize by saying that writing suggesting competence represents:

1. A tendency to depend on the self-evident and the cliché and thus for the writer to write uninformative discourse.
2. A tendency either to make the organization obvious or to write aimlessly without a plan.
3. A limitation in the range of words and thus a dependence on the clichés and colloquialisms most available.
4. An ability to use mechanics correctly or incorrectly in proportion to the plainness or complexity of the style.
5. A general unawareness of choices that affect style and thus an inability to control the effects a writer may seek.

D- AND E-ESSAYS

We will not methodically analyze D- and E-papers as we have A-, B-, and C-papers. Since the writing in each represents degrees of incompetency, the characteristics can be described as the opposite of those of competent writing. We can, however, summarize general tendencies that mark inferior writing:

1. A tendency to exploit the obvious either because of lack of understanding, inability to read, failure to grapple with a topic, or, in many instances, lack of interest. The substance of essays therefore ranges from superficial to barren.
2. A tendency to wander aimlessly because of a lack of overall conception or, in some instances, to have a semblance of form without the development that makes the parts a whole.
3. A tendency to play safe with words, using ones the writer

ordinarily speaks or the ones the writer can spell. These tendencies place obvious limits upon the writer to vary the expression.

4. A frequent inability to make careful distinctions between periods, commas, and semicolons, although some writers in these categories can write correct sentences if they keep structures simple. The incidence of error, however, is high.

5. Either a tendency to write highly convoluted sentences that are close to the rapid associations of our thoughts before we straighten them out or a tendency to play safe by avoiding the sentence elements that invite error (introductory modifiers, embedding, coordination, and various other sentence-combining techniques).

In stating these generalizations, I have intentionally excluded the special problems of bilingual students and of speakers of nonstandard dialects and have not used examples from their writing. The writing of these students can be atypical in many ways. In content, it may be mature and perceptive, although lacking in formal control. In language, it may be vigorous, although lacking in consistency of tone and usage. In style, it may be moving, although fragmentary and error-ridden. Often the psychological barriers to writing are so strong that special emphasis must be given to encouragement, whenever and wherever possible. Because the motivation of many of these students is especially strong, they can make remarkable improvement in a short time, given a compatible teacher-student relationship.

In choosing samples of D- and E-writing, I have intentionally not chosen those that are error-ridden. Those are easy to account for. It is more difficult to judge papers that pose few mechanical problems and may even reveal considerable involvement on the part of the writer. I will therefore admit that a grade of D on the following essay may well be controversial. The running commentary and concluding remarks will attempt to support that evaluation. It should be noted that the essay was written in class late in the quarter. One of the topics asked students to respond in their own way to the lyrics of "The Sound of Silence" by Paul Simon. Students were given the text.

D-Essay

This song is so meaningful, expressive, or something, that it's really hard to know where to start—I mean it's about *us*, people and the way we are, and yet actually it's talking about the void we've made in and amongst ourselves.

Initial signs of being overwhelmed emotionally.

To being, "Hello darkness my old friend,/ I've come to talk with you again. . ." Darkness is a shield that can temporarily cover up irrelevant things which we've made seem relevant, and, with these obstacles put aside, expose what life really is, *raw.*

What this means is a mystery. Corresponds to Stanza 1 of the song.

"In restless dreams I walked alone. . .". The vision comes in a dream, and the vision is Truth, so it remains within the sound of silence. The sound of silence being the void. There's a neon light flashing, piercing the raw life and showing all the people there conversing, with no one really saying anything or even hearing each other's empty words—perhaps that's why. Our mechanical movements persist, but amidst all the mechanics the void remains and people know it's there, although many don't understand what it is that *isn't* there—that's the sound of the silence: the *presence* of an unfulfillment, I guess I could say.

Comments on Stanzas 2 and 3. Some meaning emerges, but not clearly enough to connect the thought with what has gone before.

Then Simon says: People, you don't realize that the silence is growing louder and louder; let me *reach* you and make you understand—but the silence, that awful frustrating silence, remains. Instead, we people, caught by our new gods—our loud, flashy, irrelevant cover-ups—ignore the silence.

Relates to Stanza 4. Relatively clear statement.

We have created ourselves and created our tenements, and these symbols of the silence, caught up by the neon Godess, are saying: "See what you've done, Man; you were *supposed* to be like *this*. . ." But you don't *have* to be—hear the sound of silence. But we—Mankind—*don't* hear. Individuals do—Paul Simon heard the sound of silence, and could put it into words.

Relates to Stanza 5, the last stanza of the poem. First two sentences totally unclear.

It's everything that we're *capable* of being, as man to man, and everything that we still *aren't*—but it's there waiting for us to *be.*

Afterthoughts and conclusions, but no resolution of what remains essentially puzzling.

> The sound of silence comes on stronger in
> the darkness: it strikes through like naked light.
> The exposure of men to themselves and each oth-
> er, stripped of what they've hidden themselves be-
> hind. I said before that the darkness is a shield—
> actually I mean that it's a shield from our neon
> Gods. Just as we force our neon Gods to shield us
> from the sound of silence.

There is no reason to conclude that the young woman who wrote this essay is incompetent as a writer, but this particular theme (the important distinction between the person and the performance) suggests incompetence. The opening paragraph indicates that she is overwhelmed by the lyrics of the song, and she never quite recovers. Further, it is not a matter of knowing "where to start"; it's a matter of not knowing where to go. Even though many writers are tempted to do a stanza-by-stanza response, that approach needs a clear line of thought running throughout the commentary. Once this student begins, words flow without a sense of direction or organizational pattern. The result is a series of impressions, many of them vague and elusive, and for the most part meaningless.

Very early in the quarter, an instructor assigned the following topic as the subject of an in-class essay: "Think of an object or activity and describe it first positively, then negatively, being specific and detailed in both descriptions." It should be noted that the assignment has a built-in pitfall, not intentional, of course, but a pitfall nevertheless. I refer to the generality of the topic. It has to be narrowed—focused—in order to be treated successfully. A rephrasing of the topic might help those students who fail to recognize what they have to do in the preparatory stage, as this student obviously did not.

E-Essay

Working is a very good way to make money, but there is more behind work than money. Money is earned, therefore the value of money is learned. Kids learn fast how to work both for and with other people, which will be very valuable to

Paper begins with a truism, tries to be aphoristic, then concludes with two more self-evident statements.

them in future life. It is a good way for teens to become more independent of their parents so that the eventual break will be less difficult.

Work can also be a restraining burden. It is hard to plan a night out not knowing whether you will have to work or not. At times pressure is very great on employees. These pressures can build and be unbearable and cause ulcers or a nervous breakdown. Work can also get in the way of school and lower grades.

The example given in Sentence 2 may illustrate an inconvenience, but it is not quite a convincing example of a "restraining burden." Remainder of short paragraph treats two additional topics.

As one of the managers at Herfy's in the district, I see these things happening every day. I see both the good and the bad and am convinced that the good outweighs the bad one hundred percent.

Paragraph 3 is intended no doubt to be summary and conclusion for a paper that needs neither.

Some teachers might be so pleased to see complete sentences and correctly spelled words that they would want to claim that this paper "suggests competence." But such a claim would have to ignore completely the content and style. The thought is about as empty and vapid as we might imagine any statement on the subject. There is only one specific reference in the 168 words: "As one of the managers at Herfy's in the district . . . ." All of the other statements are generalizations, illogically strung together.

Stylistically, the sentences are cramped. If we can equate the length of the essay with the 45 or 50 minutes allowed to write it, the writer averages about four minutes per sentence. Certainly there is no flow. This kind of crabbed prose should not represent a passing standard for college work, despite the fact that the writing of students in basic writing classes may show qualities that are far more obviously substandard. Of course, the truth is that students in those classes often do have something to say and can express their thoughts with a high degree of fluency. What they lack is control and an acquaintance with standard forms. Thus, their writing appears far more disorderly. Yet their deficiencies may be more easily addressed than those of the writer of "Working," for it would seem that this writer will not show much improvement unless he removes the psychological barrier that is inhibiting expression. This is the kind of student who needs pre-writing exercises, especially those that will release him from his uptightness about writing.

Failure, frustration, and desperation often lead to plagiarism. They are more often the cause than deliberate dishonesty. I am therefore inclined to view plagiarism more as a psychological problem than a moral issue.

Most teachers respond to plagiarism with indignation. It is an affront—a kind of insult insinuating that the teacher can't differentiate one person's writing from another's. The emotional reaction is quite natural. If we are going to seek a remedy for plagiarism rather than just punish it, we do need to set feelings aside in order to find out why someone has plagiarized. The matter has to be talked out, and the student's embarrassment may be cause enough for that person to conclude that doing one's own work is a better course of action. If we can convince someone of that fact, we have made a learning situation out of a dilemma that otherwise remains unsolved by a failing grade.

We should also recognize that some plagiarism grows out of ignorance and carelessness, especially in doing a paper based on library sources. Students fail to use quotation marks in taking notes; they fail to paraphrase and then use their notes almost verbatim to write their papers. This kind of plagiarism can be offset by teaching the proper uses of summary and paraphrase.

Even though plagiarism is endemic to writing courses, the less preachment the better. Too much warning sets up a challenge for some individuals. There are always those who enjoy violating the law as long as they don't get caught. Positive expectations are better, and preventive measures can make plagiarism more trouble than it is worth. Students who want to learn will do their own work. We should not set the tone of a class in terms of those who don't want to learn. When we threaten, we usually worry those who have least cause for concern. Callous plagiarists are not deterred by warnings. The one virtue they seem to have is that they confess when the jig is up. And that may be a sign of hope.

·   ·   ·

In analyzing and evaluating samples of writing in this chapter, I have tried to make clear the assumptions on which I have based the choice of grades. It should also be clear that if one begins with a radically different value system, the grades will be different. Where readers are drawn from different sources to read student papers for credit, equivalency, placement or advanced placement, exemption, or proficiency—group-grading situations where uniformity of standards is especially important—it is necessary first to brief readers on criteria for judgment and then practice-grade until the discrepancies have been minimized. A similar kind of exercise should be a part of any orientation program for new teachers or of any class for students preparing to teach English. That kind of discussion of values is the best measure against continuing grade inflation.

If the grades of A, B, C, D, and E are defined in terms of relative competency and incompetency and students are familiar with those definitions, the grade on an essay should be read only as a generalization about the student's performance. All of the particulars, designed to help, should be incorporated in the marks and comments. These are of little value unless the student tries to respond to them. Revising and rewriting are as much a part of the writing process as preparing and shaping and editing.

Attitudes toward revision, on the part of both teachers and students, vary widely. Experienced writers know the necessity of rewriting. Inexperienced ones find something distasteful about returning to a job that they consider finished, particularly when it means revising or rewriting a theme that is returned a week after it was written. They find it difficult to warm again to the subject. Yet that very cooling off provides the kind of detachment we need to tamper with our own prose—altering a word, reconstructing a sentence, recasting a paragraph. We have to emphasize that reworking one's own prose is far more meaningful than responding to any handbook or workbook exercises. My own experience indicates that students rather typically resist revision and won't do it unless they are required to do so, but when they are required to make changes they realize the value and often say that being "forced" to reconsider their choices was one of the most useful parts of the course.

We cannot automatically assume that students know how to revise simply because we ask them to. At times, I have given students an opportunity to revise their papers in class *before* they turn them in at the end of the period. There is some reluctance to mess up the neat appearance of a page, but, beyond that, some of them simply do not know what to do. They lack a repertory of choices. For that reason, small-group critiquing often helps. One student may be able to provide a solution for another, for essentially revision entails finding solutions to writing problems or finding better ways of saying the same thing. Doing revisions in class on the day essays are returned is also another way to overcome the rather casual attitude many students take when they have to work on their own at home.

Conferences are especially useful for teaching revision. In that setting, teacher and student together can explore possibilities. Part of the dialogue can be demonstration: "Put the paper aside, and tell me what you are trying to say." Part of it can be asking questions: "Do you know the difference between 'effect' and 'affect'?" A teacher can often accomplish in 10 minutes of conference what hundreds of written comments might never do. The simple reason is that the informality of talking permits both teacher and student to focus on the crucial problem and find out what the student needs to know. The conference and the revising process can be further aided if all students keep their papers in a folder. Then, teacher and student can make comparisons. They can see what has been happening, whether any response has been occurring, and whether any internalization seems to be taking place. When internalization of a principle finally occurs, the troubling symptoms go away.

In an art form like film-making, we know that editing and revising cannot be dismissed as superfluous, for they are an integral part of the whole process. In fact, what we eventually see on the screen is not what was filmed, but what was edited. The same should be true of writing, despite the fact that we go about the two processes in different ways. Nevertheless, more and more we should emphasize that the job of writing is not done until we have moved through all of the stages from pre-writing to rewriting. Rewriting is one sure way of learning to write better.

14

The Realities of the Job

In reading the applications of candidates for admission to the teacher-preparation program at the University of Washington and later interviewing the students, I have been amazed at their naiveté and lack of perception of what the job of teaching English actually entails. When individuals say, "I want to be an English teacher," they ought to have some notion what the realities of the job are, not necessarily to discourage them from what they hope to do, but to remind them that the job of teaching English, like many other ones, has its rewards and its disappointments. I want to comment on a few of the realities of teaching composition, although some of these apply to teaching in general. They are reminders that discouragements and failures may not be personal; they may simply be indigenous to the job.

1. *Teaching writing is hard work.*

Not only is teaching writing hard work, it is a real challenge to the inventiveness of a teacher, because this kind of teaching is done best not by talking about writing (or style or structure), but by leading others to discover what is happening as this process occurs and by that means to learn better how to control what is happening. Teaching writing therefore requires preparation; it requires study and expertise.

Teaching writing also requires patience, because improvement is not always apparent. If, as I have suggested, progress occurs more by leaps and bounds than by steady steps, some teachers may not see the results of their efforts. In a few months, one teacher cannot hope to make up for years of neglect. But that teacher can create an awareness of values, make students conscious of their strengths (their weaknesses seem always to be present), and provide practice. A lack of patience and the desire to see rapid change prompt many teachers to turn to prescriptions and gimmicks. Even though results become more readily visible by such means, they may be doing nothing more than altering surface features. Students commonly revert to old habits once they are out of the English classroom. The aim of teaching writing should be to create new habits.

2. *At times, everybody gets tired of reading papers.*

Boredom with reading student themes is proportionate to the amount of dull writing a teacher gets; the dull writing, in turn, will be proportionate to the students' own interest in what they are doing. Since reading papers is endemic to teaching writing, the teacher's responsibility is to see that topics actually motivate students to write, that they have choices in what they can write about, and that they are writing because they have something to say, not because they are being pressed. What we get in writing is often what we invite.

3. *We are not teaching writing unless students are writing.*

It follows—or so we usually think—that if students are writing we must be reading. The simple fact is that staying ahead of the writing is the most burdensome part of teaching writing, particularly if the teacher makes the kind of analytical comments I have suggested and does not merely "correct." The next hard fact is that the student loads of some teachers, especially at the high school level, make thoughtful consideration of every essay almost an impossible task. The usual solution is to reduce writing assignments or eliminate them altogether rather than find alternatives to reading and evaluating every paper, even though those alternatives may be a compromise with ideal conditions.

For instance, as an alternative, if all students wrote twelve essays during a term, the teacher might read and evaluate every third one on a staggered schedule. The ones in between might be read by other students. Or they might be kept in a folder, and when three have accumulated the student might be asked to submit the best one. Or formal papers might be interspersed with journal writing so that the journal becomes a practice book and generative device. Or, if the class is converted into a kind of writing workshop, the teacher might be available to read and respond to whatever a student wants read at a particular time. Or all papers might be read but with the clear understanding that the teacher's comments will be selective—organization one time, voice another, diction another. I once had a teaching assistant who wrote more in response to the students than they wrote for her. She could not be persuaded to do less, even though I tried to point out that there is such a thing as doing too much. She eventually had to quit in a state of nervous exhaustion. She helped neither her students nor herself.

4. *We have to find ways to cope with numbers.*

Books on teaching and curriculum guides always talk about individualized instruction. It is practically the standard cliché of the profession, more often preached than practiced, however. Experienced teachers, of course, share that ideal, but they also know that learning to teach well in the schools and colleges means learning to cope with group situations and trying to get students to participate in the process of learning. Teaching composition has a special advantage because commenting on a student's paper is always an individualized response. Making helpful comments is one of the most important things a composition instructor does.

5. *Failure of a student is not necessarily the teacher's failure.*

The notion that a student's failure is the teacher's failure is based on the belief that the teacher's responsibility is to teach students, while overlooking the fact that students also have responsibilities to study and learn. New teachers, sometimes shiny with evangelical zeal, eventually learn to recognize that students can fail for a number of reasons quite beyond their control. Through the writing itself, teachers of writing often become aware of personal and social problems that students are struggling with. The temptation is to confuse themselves with parents, counselors, preachers, psychiatrists, and confidants and try to solve problems. That temptation ought to be resisted. It is a mixing of roles. Granted, we have talked about writing as a form of behavior, but becoming a specialist in the teaching of writing does not make one a specialist in all forms of human behavior. Sensitivity to problems may be as much solution as some students need.

Recognizing that students sometimes fail for reasons beyond a teacher's control does not deny that teachers can be negligent and inefficient. In fact, if large numbers of students do poor work, a teacher needs to consider if the work has been overly demanding or if students have been bored by a lack of challenge or if the teacher's own problems have become the source of the difficulty. When the reciprocal relation between student and teacher is broken because one or the other neglects responsibilities, failure or poor performance can occur.

6. *Bluffing on the teacher's part usually doesn't work—or at least doesn't work consistently.*

In the post-Salinger age, students are remarkably good at spotting phonies. Bluffing represents anything from trying to cover up for being unprepared to issuing threats that students know a teacher cannot carry out. The threats usually concern penalties for absences, late papers, required revisions, plagiarism, and particular errors, like misspellings, fragments, and comma splices. If a threat is unenforceable or if enforcing it means that half of the students are going to fail, then the teacher had better look to alternative and more reasonable ways of maintaining discipline. Teacher and students should be working cooperatively.

7. *A teacher of writing is not completely autonomous.*

In a sense, no teacher is completely autonomous, but teachers who are part of the growth process that learning to write represents have a responsibility to contribute their part. In some public school systems, teachers may be part of a coordinated curriculum. In some colleges, teachers may be required to follow a standardized program including common texts, syllabuses, and departmental examinations. The degree of independence a teacher has depends upon the place and setting. Unfortunately, many teachers are more anxious to work against the system than to see it work. If it is not workable, then efforts should be made to change the system, not to subvert it.

8. *Teaching composition is often considered a service function.*

In academe, a service function is a lowly function. In English studies, especially in colleges, teaching expository writing is considered menial, despite the fact that most of the hours of the departmental schedule may be devoted to writing classes. Freshman composition is something to graduate from, not to specialize in. Those who teach composition exclusively are usually second-class citizens in the department. They are low in rank; they are low on the salary scale.

It should be quickly added that college composition teachers have been in part responsible for their own dilemma. They have been content to do their jobs, but often in an unprofessional way. They have seen little reason to study their discipline or engage in research projects related to their concerns. They have exempted themselves from publication. But those conditions do not need to prevail. Teaching composition should be given the professional recognition it deserves as an integral part of English studies at all levels.

The organization that has done most to establish the professionalism of composition teaching is the Conference on College Composition and Communication, which meets annually in the spring of the year. Its quarterly journal *College Composition and Communication* is a major source of current thinking on matters of composition and rhetoric. Teachers of composition who take the subject seriously ought to read it. It will reveal what a vital activity the teaching of composition can be, all of which leads to several realities of a positive nature.

9. *The teaching of composition is an ever-expanding discipline.*

One of the appealing things about the teaching of composition is that it seems to carry one constantly into related spheres of activity. One of the most recent that I know of is designing courses for men and women in prisons. The psychological and sociological dimensions of this planning are highly important. Other specialties include second-language learning, teaching composition to speakers of nonstandard dialects, technical writing (I know of several courses designed especially for policemen), business writing, testing (equivalency, placement, and proficiency), training teachers of writing, writing laboratories, reading development, high school/college liaison, summer institutes for experienced teachers, rhetorical theory, linguistics, and stylistics. The list undoubtedly could be lengthened. My point is that teaching composition is neither repetitive nor dead end. It is only to those who are unwilling to commit themselves to new study and untested areas.

10. *The teaching of composition throughout the country and the general state of literacy could be immensely improved if more teachers knew what they were doing.*

I write this statement optimistically, not cynically. Teachers will readily admit that they are unprepared to teach composition. When they discover that there are things to understand and do, they go about the job in a different way, often encouraging other teachers to take a course or read a book or article. That cooperative effort is important because an isolated teacher in a particular grade doing a good job is not enough. As we discussed earlier, students need the intuitive confidence of acquired learning throughout their school years. When we get that, we may even be spared the next exposé of illiteracy that seems to come in the press with varying degrees of intensity about every decade.

11. *The teaching of composition can be pleasurable and rewarding.*

The rewards depend to a great extent on the teacher's attitude. If teaching composition is only a chore to be done as perfunctorily as possible, then the experience is likely to be routine. I recently saw a TV commericial during which one woman said to another, "I teach sailing." The background noise and the actress's faulty enunciation caused me to hear with some surprise, "I teach failing." I came to a quick realization that no one would ever say such a thing, but then in a somewhat didactic turn of mind, I thought how true the statement was nevertheless. Some teachers teach failing. They expect failure. They dare some students to succeed. Positive expectations in teaching composition are crucial. When students know there is hope, they are remarkably generous in their response.

The rewards of teaching composition are often the pleasures of being able to see tangible results as time passes, making expression possible for some individual who seemed mute, experiencing a new fluency in some students and a genuine flare in others. It's axiomatic that some students achieve excellence in spite of their teachers. Others need teachers, however. Teachers who have been a part of a student's achievement have a true sense of their role.

.　　.　　.

Having reached this point, we should realize that writing involves more than transcribing words on paper. Writing involves clarifying values, assessing knowledge, organizing experience, questioning, defining, and, finally, finding words and arrangements that will make the thoughts and expressions of one person clear to another. If we are simply overwhelmed by the demands of teaching these things, we will do as so many others have done before: we will simply ask students to write. And they will hesitate, flounder, question, and struggle as so many others have done before. Teachers with new confidence about what they are doing can help students move toward certainty in what they are doing

Obviously, this book could have been much longer; it could have included more how-to-do-it information. But I have intentionally tried to keep it brief, open-ended, and, above all, readable. I hope some of its premises prompt questions and discussion, even argument. But, especially, I hope somebody becomes a better composition teacher for having thought about what is involved when we teach writing.

Coda

This is a brief addition to indicate where an interested reader might go from here. I would like to recommend only a limited number of sources that will help someone find a direction.

For a thorough bibliographical coverage and discussion of various approaches to teaching composition, Tate's bibliography is an indispensable source:

> Tate, Gary, ed. *Teaching Composition: 10 Bibliographical Essays*. Fort Worth, Texas: Texas Christian University Press, 1976.

I have already referred to *College Composition and Communication* as the leading periodical on the teaching of writing. Since 1975 (covering 1973 and 1974), the May issue of that journal has included an annotated bibliography of research and writing about the teaching of composition, prepared by Richard Larson. A combined volume for a five-year period (1973–1977) has been approved for publication. It will be available from the National Council of Teachers of English. The *Rhetoric Society*

Quarterly contains extensive bibliographies on more specialized topics in rhetoric.

Besides *CCC*, the following periodicals regularly include articles on writing and the teaching of writing: *College English, The English Journal, Language Arts, Research in the Teaching of English, English Education, Freshman English News, Teaching English in the Two-Year College, The CEA Forum,* numerous affiliate publications of the National Council of Teachers of English, and a rapidly growing number of newsletters representing special interests and approaches. For instance, *The WLA Newsletter* (Writing as a Liberating Activity) is published at Findlay College, Ohio, by Richard Gebhardt; *CLAC* (Conference on Language Attitudes and Composition) is edited at Portland State University, Oregon.

Each year, NCTE publishes a catalog of publications entitled *Resources for English and the Language Arts.* It includes various publications of the Council, available to members at special prices.

One hopes that a new attitude of professionalism toward composition will produce more publications equal to four books of an essentially theoretical nature published during the 1970s. In chronological order, they are:

> Kinneavy, James L. *A Theory of Discourse.* Englewood Cliffs, N.J.: Prentice-Hall, 1971.
> D'Angelo, Frank. *A Conceptual Theory of Rhetoric.* Cambridge, Mass. Winthrop Publishing Co., 1975.
> Shaughnessy, Mina P. *Errors & Expectations: A Guide for the Teache₁ of Basic Writing.* New York: Oxford University Press, 1977.
> Hirsch, E. D., Jr. *The Philosophy of Composition.* Chicago: University of Chicago Press, 1977.

To add more would begin to overwhelm, as bibliographies have a way of doing. The important thing is to begin somewhere. One source will almost certainly lead to another

Index